KEY WEST
IN PLAIN VIEW

PHOTOGRAPHS BY
KATHY SMITH

3dogs publishing
3dogspublishing@gmail.com
Seattle, Washington

ISBN-13: 978-0615509488 (Custom Universal)
ISBN-10: 0615509487
BISAC: Photography / Subjects & Themes / Regional

Scans by Panda Photographic Labs, Inc., Seattle, WA
In Plain View Series design by Soundview Design Studios, Edmonds, WA
Production by H. Cox

Printed on Demand

Published by 3dogs publishing, Seattle, Washington
3dogspublishing@gmail.com

ARTIST STATEMENT

I spent a few days in Key West, Florida in 1979 and returned thirty years later with my Diana camera. The Diana camera is a toy camera, circa 1960's, made entirely of plastic, including the lens! It has very limited settings and produces soft, dreamlike photographs. This time I wanted to capture the unique flavor of this historical, colorful and fun-loving city that has always lingered on my mind.

I visited the homes of Hemingway, Audubon and President Harry S. Truman. I studied the lovely architecture influenced mainly by New England and the Bahamas. Cuban cuisine and cigars are still enjoyed here. Early treasure salvagers (wreckers) made huge fortunes here and their mansions still remain as testament.

The sunset is celebrated every evening on Mallory Square with carnival-like performers. All in all, Key West is an island city like no other.

Kathy Smith

FOR ROBBIE

FOREWORD

Kathy Smith's unique approach to the art of black and white photography creates a nostalgic tour down the lane of memories in Key West. The ethereal images achieved with her Diana camera lend themselves to the philosophy that there is nowhere else quite like the Southernmost city. Daily scenes become works of art due to Kathy's practiced eye and talent with the lens. This book is a creative visual experience both for the newcomer and those who have resided here for decades. The overall effect is akin to a step back in time and place with a touch of the haunted.

I was particularly fascinated by the photo taken in Hemingway's writing studio. Upon close inspection, there is a visible aura encompassing his chair in the area where he would have been while writing. I found the slight mist visible in that photo quite mysterious since I can see no other reason for it to be in evidence. How wonderful to think he is still somewhat present in the place where he wrote seventy percent of his best work.

Linda Mendez, Manager
Hemingway Museum Bookstore
Key West, FL

KEY WEST

THE LURE OF THE SEA HAS LONG ATTRACTED THE ADVENTUROUS TO KEY WEST. EARLY SETTLERS MIGRATED FROM THE BAHAMAS TO FISH FOR CONCH. CUBANS, ONLY 90 MILES AWAY, MOVED HERE TO HARVEST SPONGES AND TO MANUFACTURE CIGARS. SPANISH PIRATES, BASED MAINLY IN CUBA, PLUNDERED TRADING SHIPS. DURING THE 1850'S LOCAL WRECKERS MADE LEGAL FORTUNES FROM SHIPWRECKED VESSELS OFF THE KEYS.

THE STREETS OF KEY WEST BEAR THE LAST NAMES OF PROMINENT CITIZENS AND RELATIVES OF THE FOUR ORIGINAL LANDOWNERS: SIMONTON, WHITEHEAD, FLEMING AND GREENE. WOMEN WERE HONORED ON A FIRST NAME BASIS WITH STREET NAMES SUCH AS CAROLINE, ELIZABETH, ANGELA AND MARGARET.

KEY WEST HAS BEEN HOME TO MANY ARTISTS AND WRITERS, NAMELY TENNESSEE WILLIAMS, ROBERT FROST AND ERNEST HEMINGWAY. OVER SIXTY DESCENDENTS OF HEMINGWAY'S ORIGINAL SIX-TOED CAT, SNOWBALL, STILL ROAM FREELY AT HIS FORMER RESIDENCE. JOHN JAMES AUDUBON DREW SKETCHES OF NATIVE WILDLIFE IN THE GARDEN OF CAPT. JOHN GEIGER. HARRY S. TRUMAN SPENT ELEVEN WORKING VACATIONS AT HIS LITTLE WHITE HOUSE HERE. EVEN THE BEATLES, AFTER BEING DIVERTED ENPLANE BY HURRICANE WEATHER IN 1964, STAYED IN KEY WEST FOR ONE NIGHT AND PLAYED IN A LOCAL HANGOUT.

KEY WEST IS ONE OF AMERICA'S MOST HAUNTED CITIES. RESIDENT GHOSTS HAVE BEEN SEEN AT MANY BUSINESSES AND GUEST HOUSES SUCH AS THE HARD ROCK CAFE, CAPT. TONY'S SALOON AND THE LA CONCHA HOTEL AND NIGHTLY GHOST TOURS TELL THEIR TALES. A LOCAL ARTIST, EUGENE OTTO, OWNED A DOLL SAID TO POSSESS EVIL POWERS. THE DOLL, ROBERT, CAN STILL BE VISITED AT THE EAST MARTELLO MUSEUM, IF YOU DARE!

ON APRIL 23, 1982 KEY WEST OFFICIALLY TRIED TO SECEDE FROM THE UNITED STATES TO FORM THE CONCH REPUBLIC. ALTHOUGH THIS ATTEMPT FIZZLED, KEY WESTERS REMAIN INDEPENDENT IN SPIRIT. THEY WARMLY WELCOME PEOPLE OF OTHER CULTURES, LIFESTYLES AND SEXUAL ORIENTATION, EMBODYING THE OFFICIAL KEY WEST CITY MOTTO: **ONE HUMAN FAMILY.**

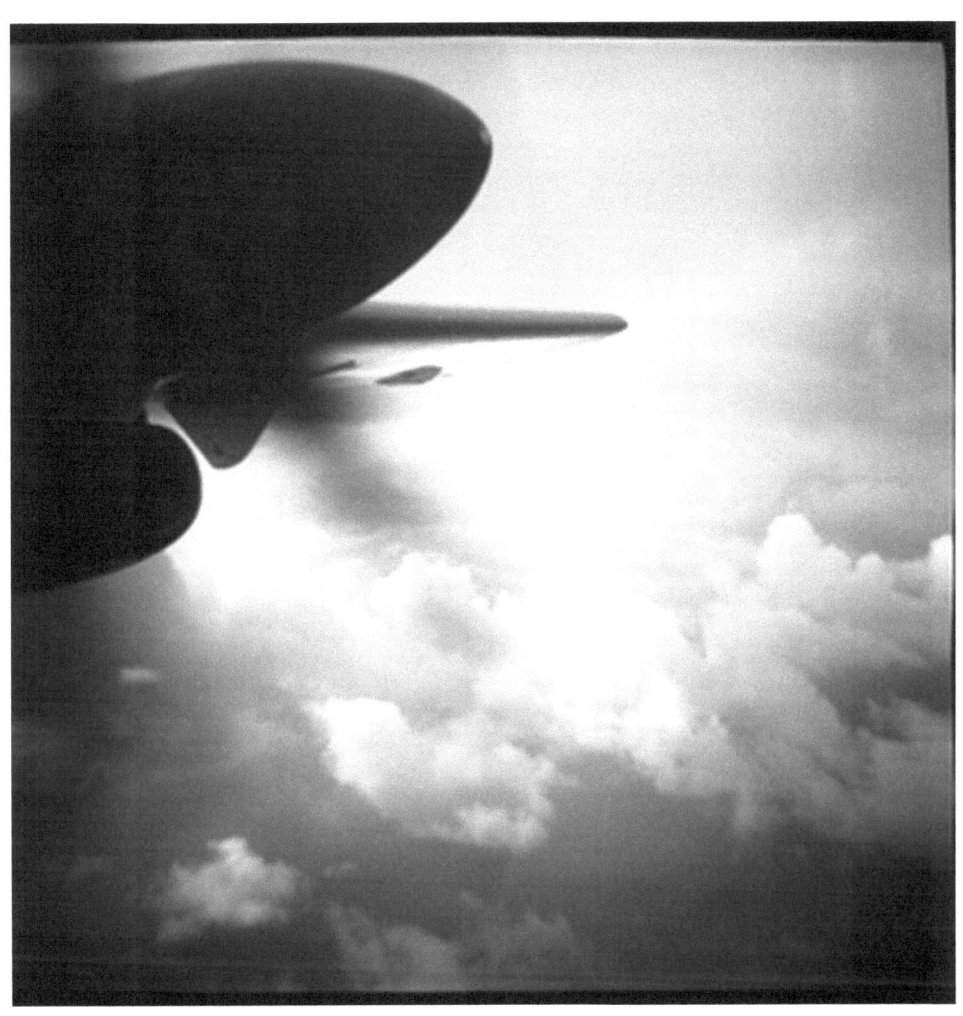

CAPE AIR FLIGHT

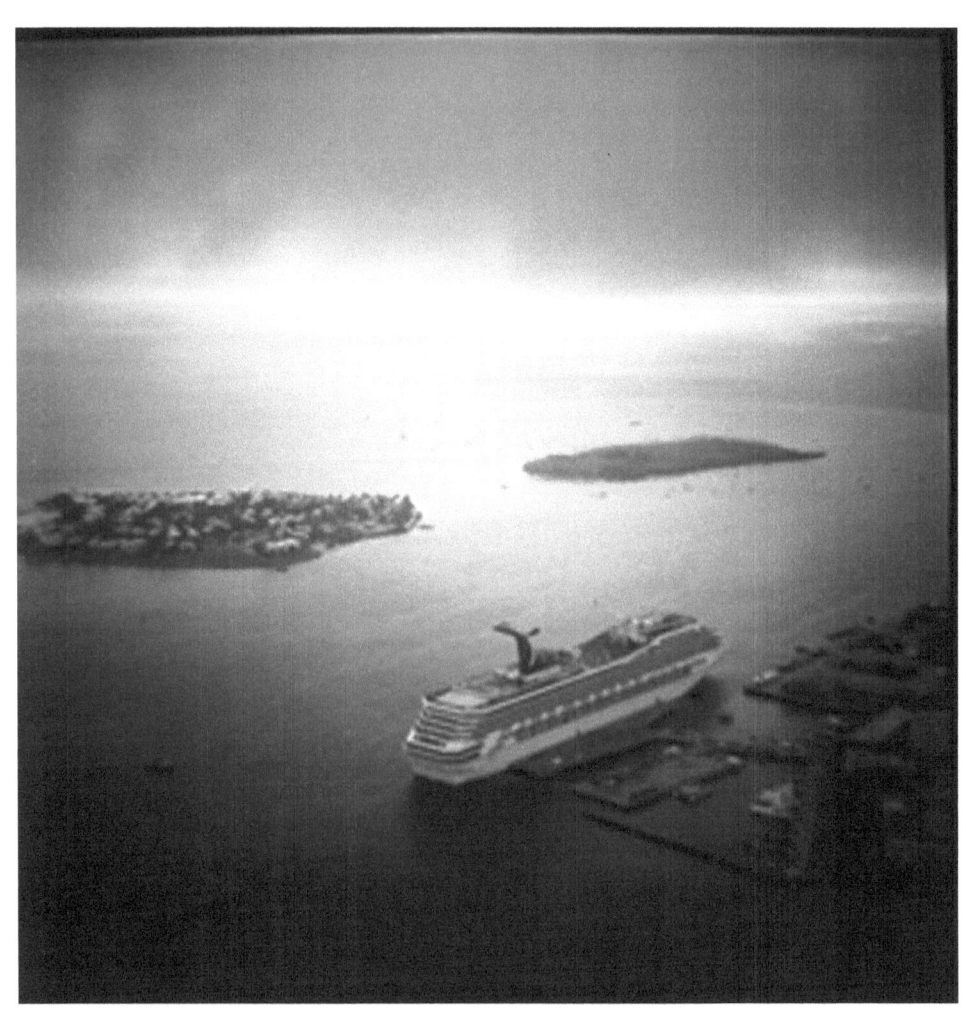

AERIAL VIEW ONE

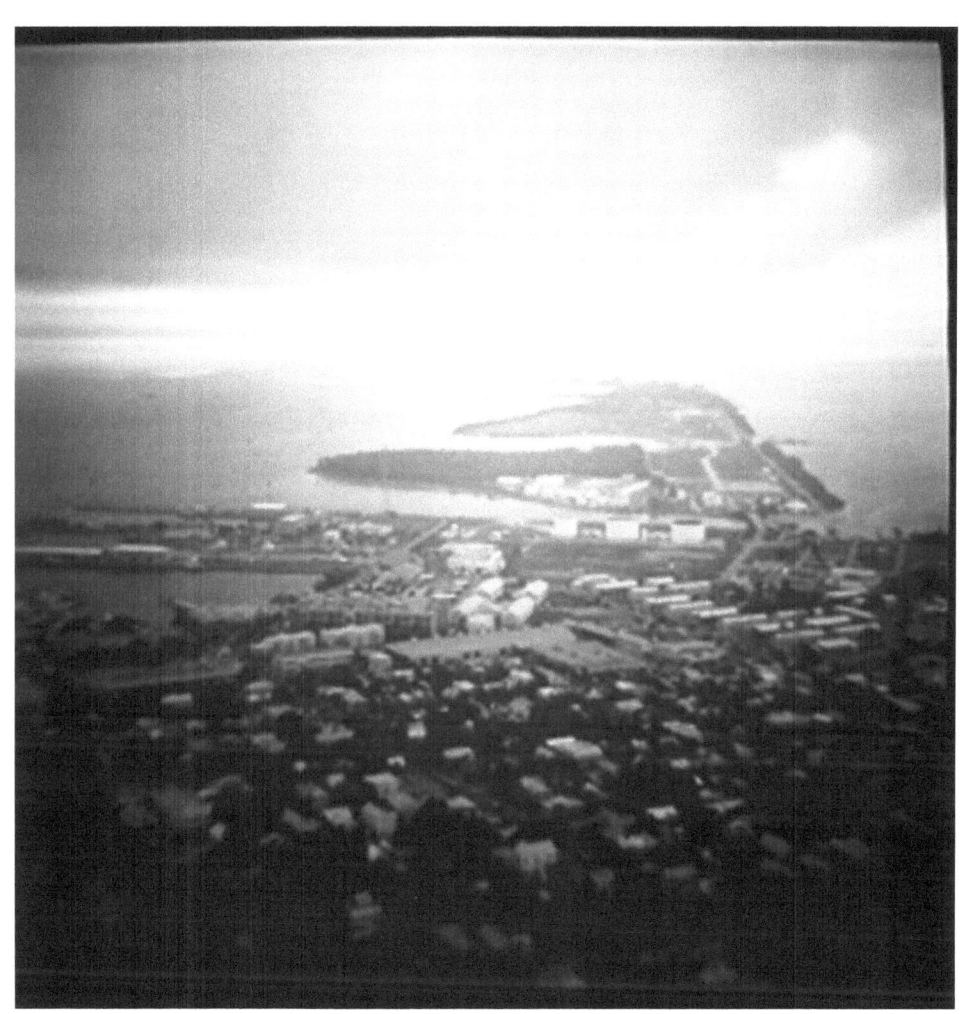

AERIAL VIEW TWO

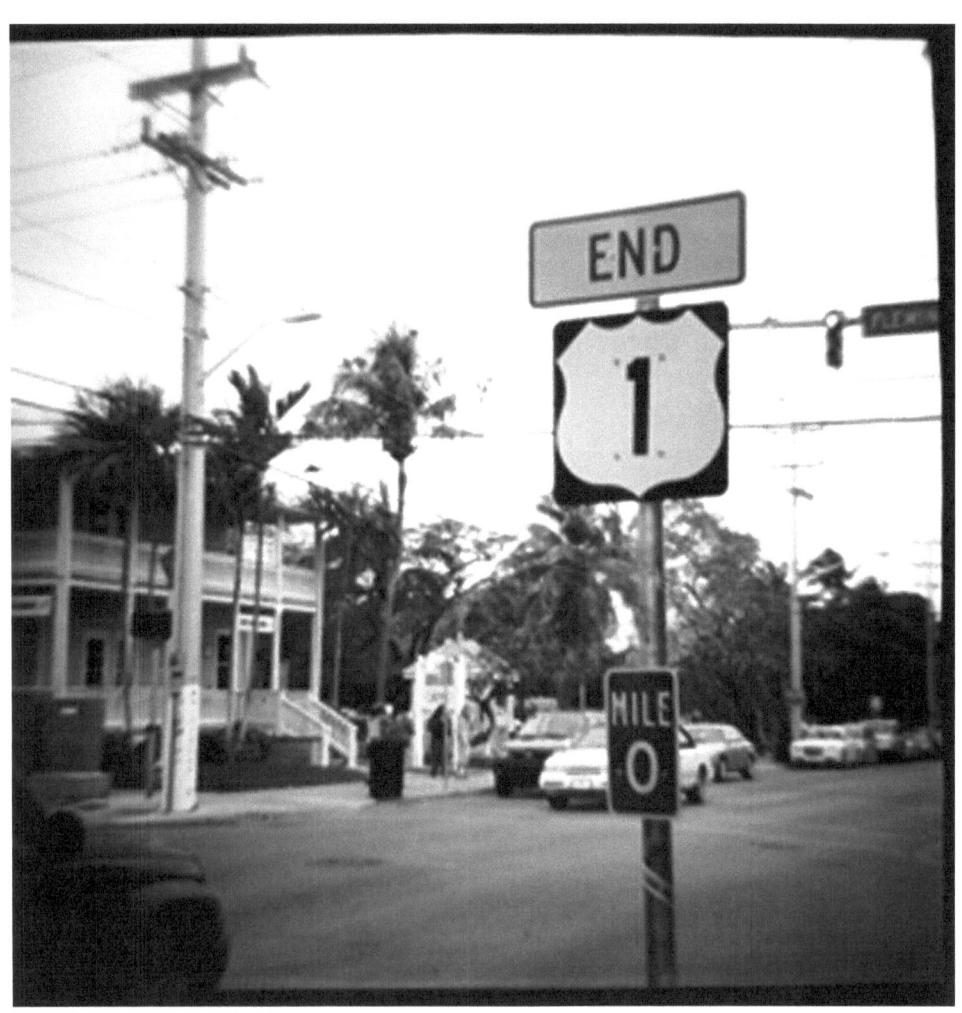

MILE MARKER 0

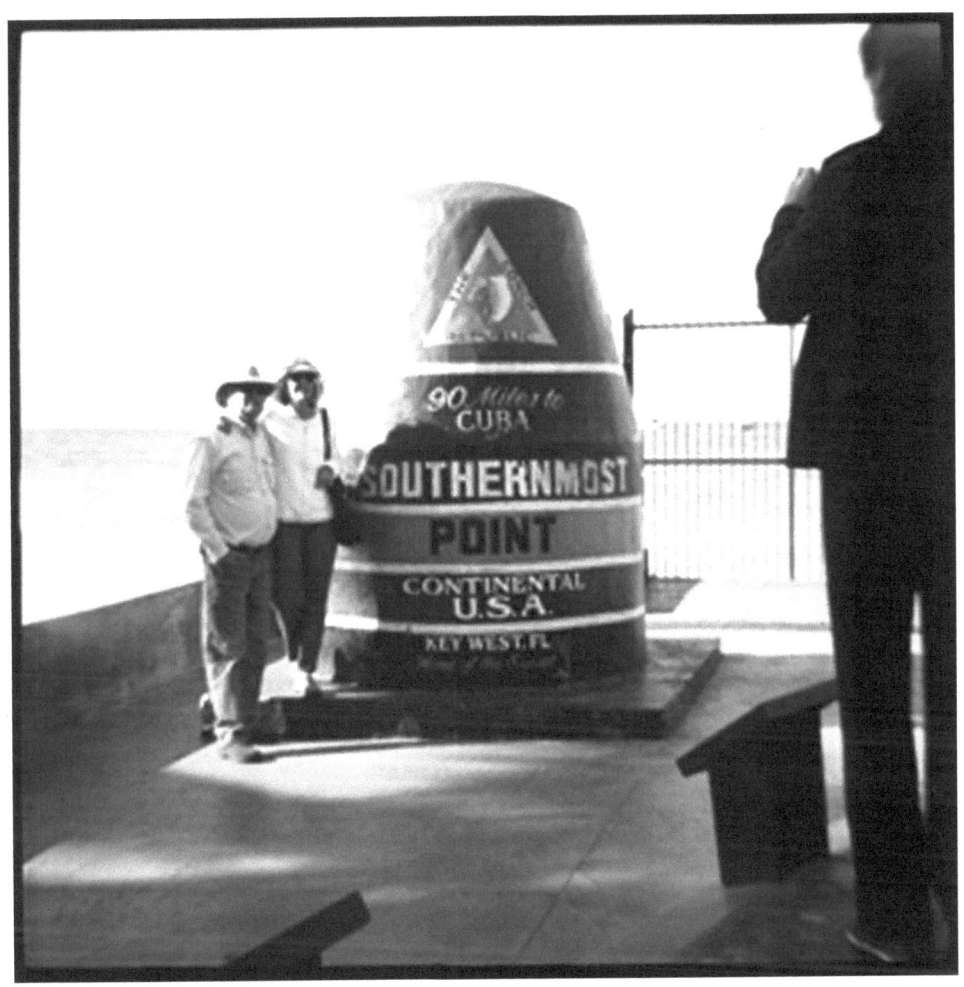

SOUTHERNMOST POINT MARKER

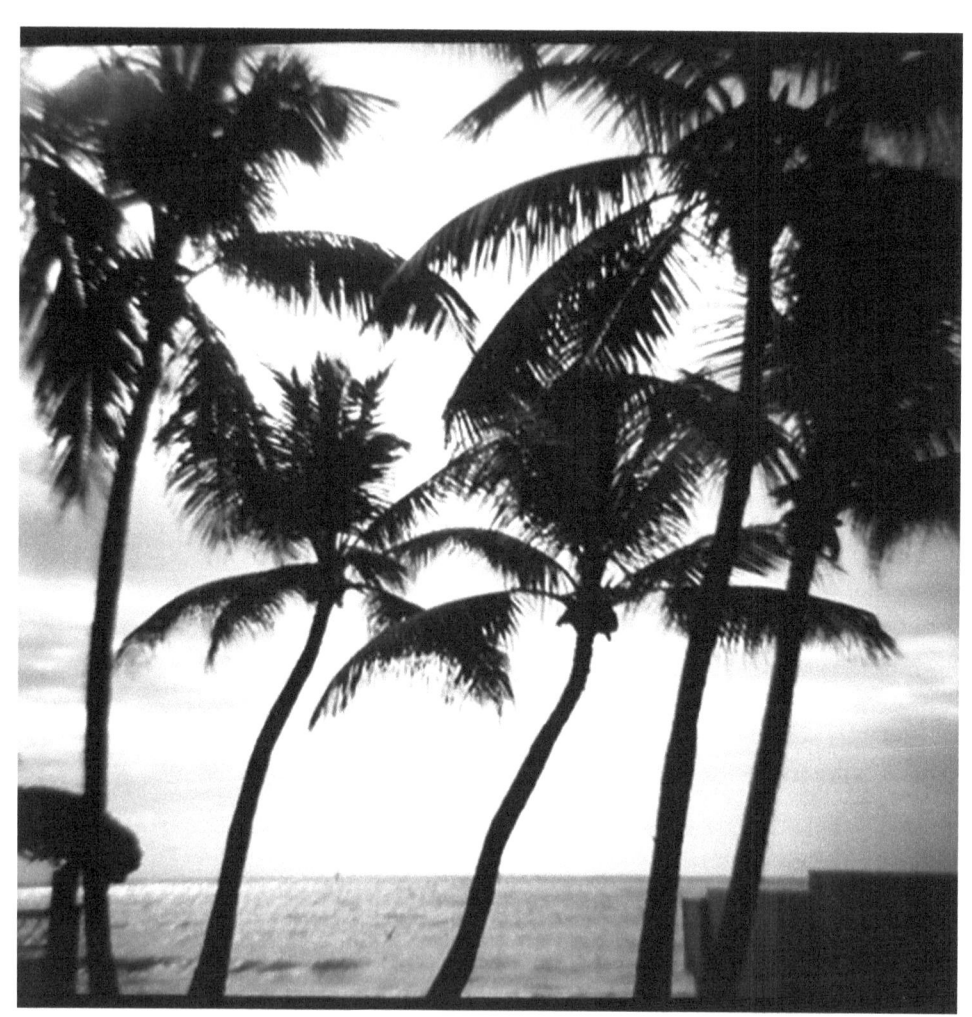

FIVE PALMS

DOG BEACH

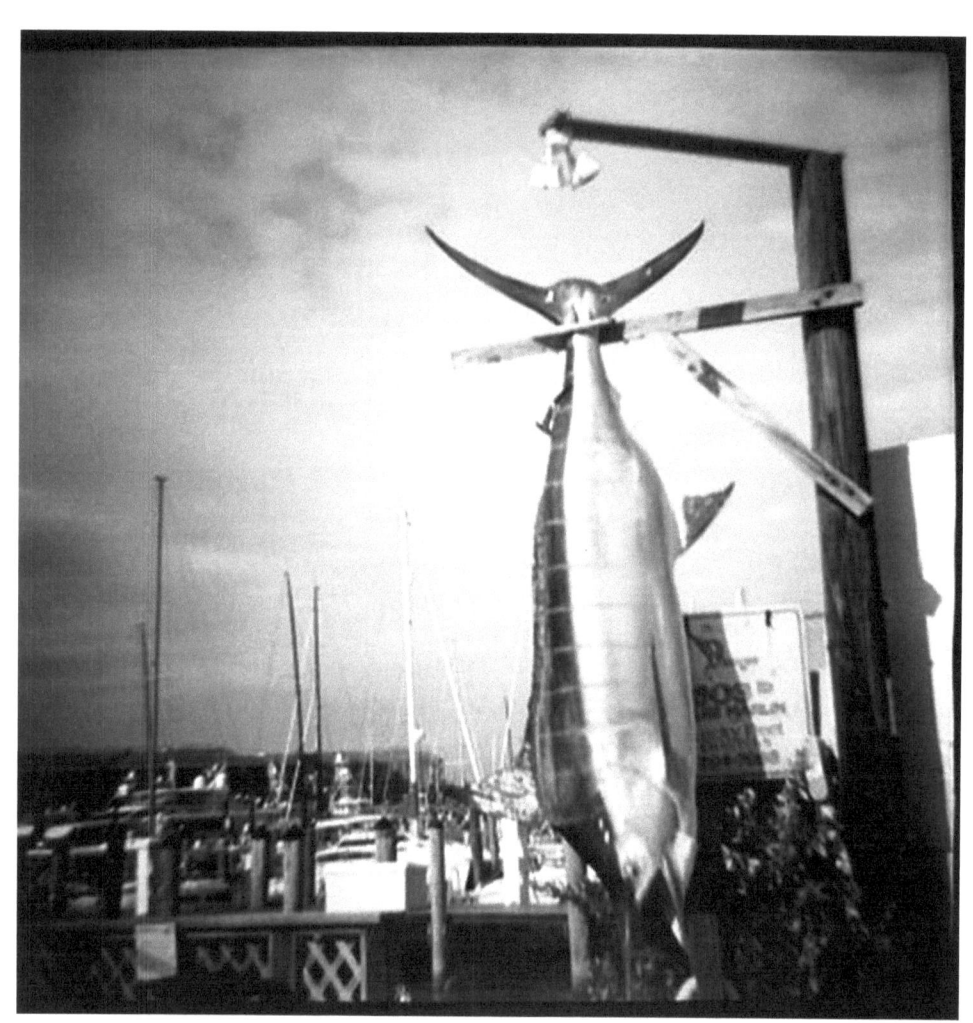

HANGING FISH

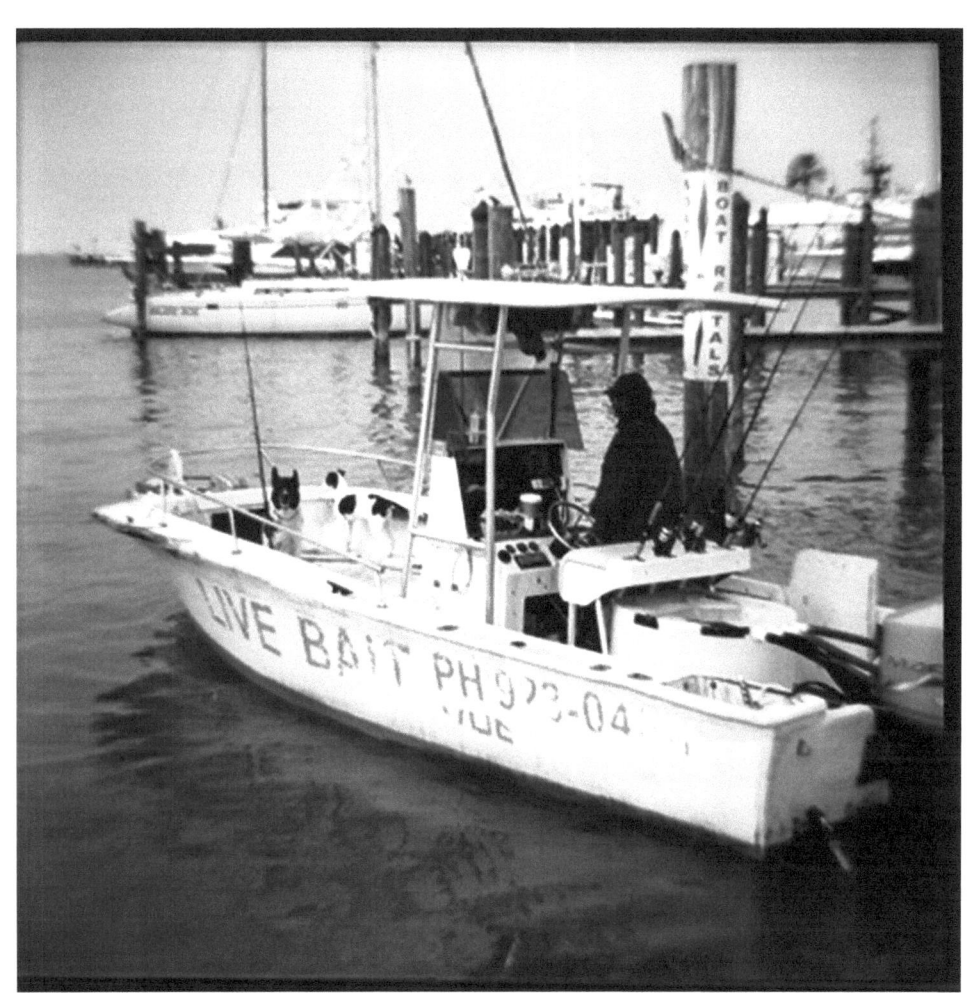

LIVE BAIT BOAT

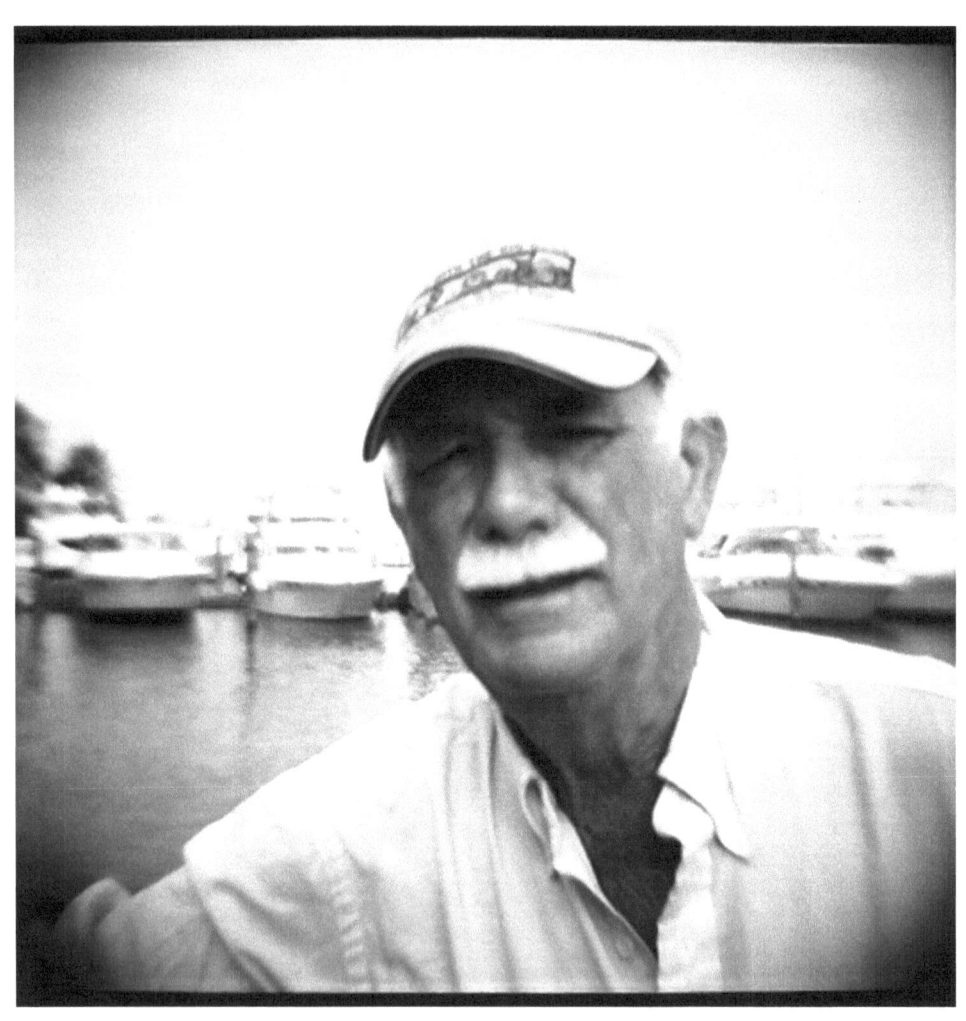

PETER
JOLLY ROVER CREW

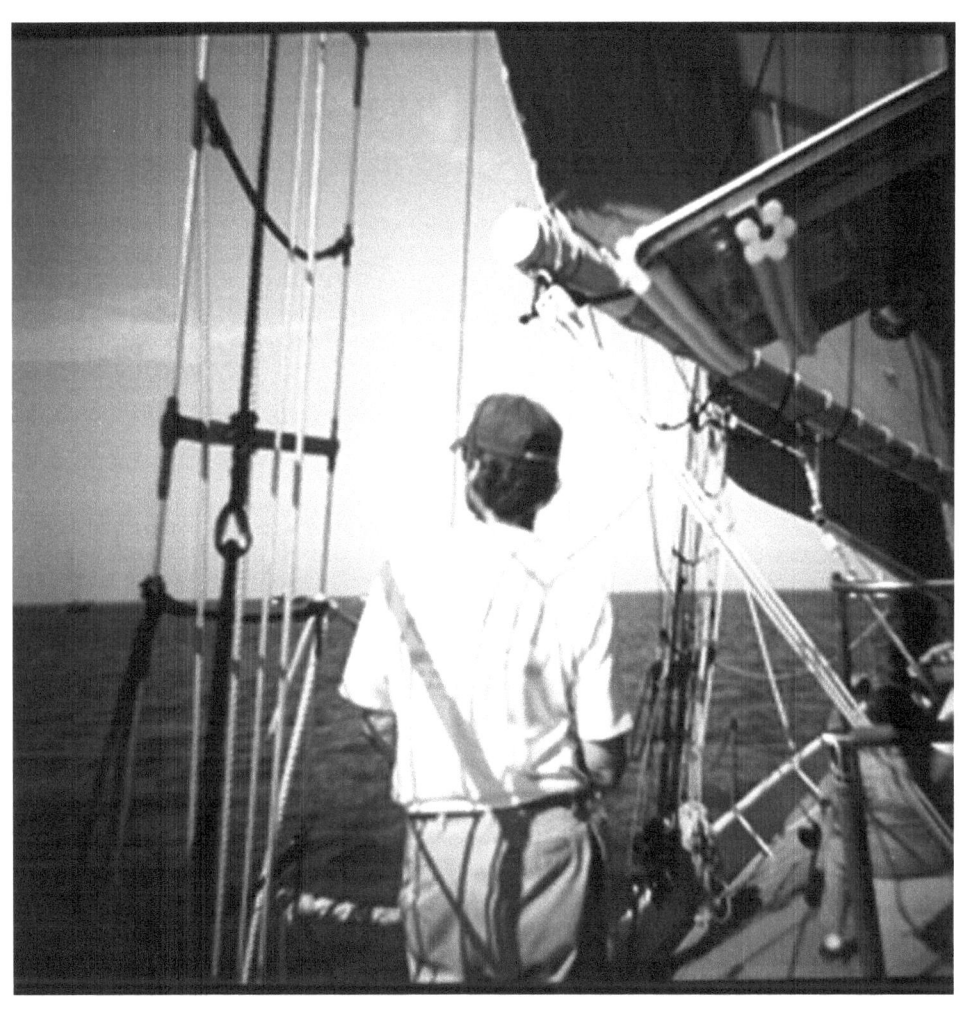

CAPTAIN RON
Aboard the Jolly Rover

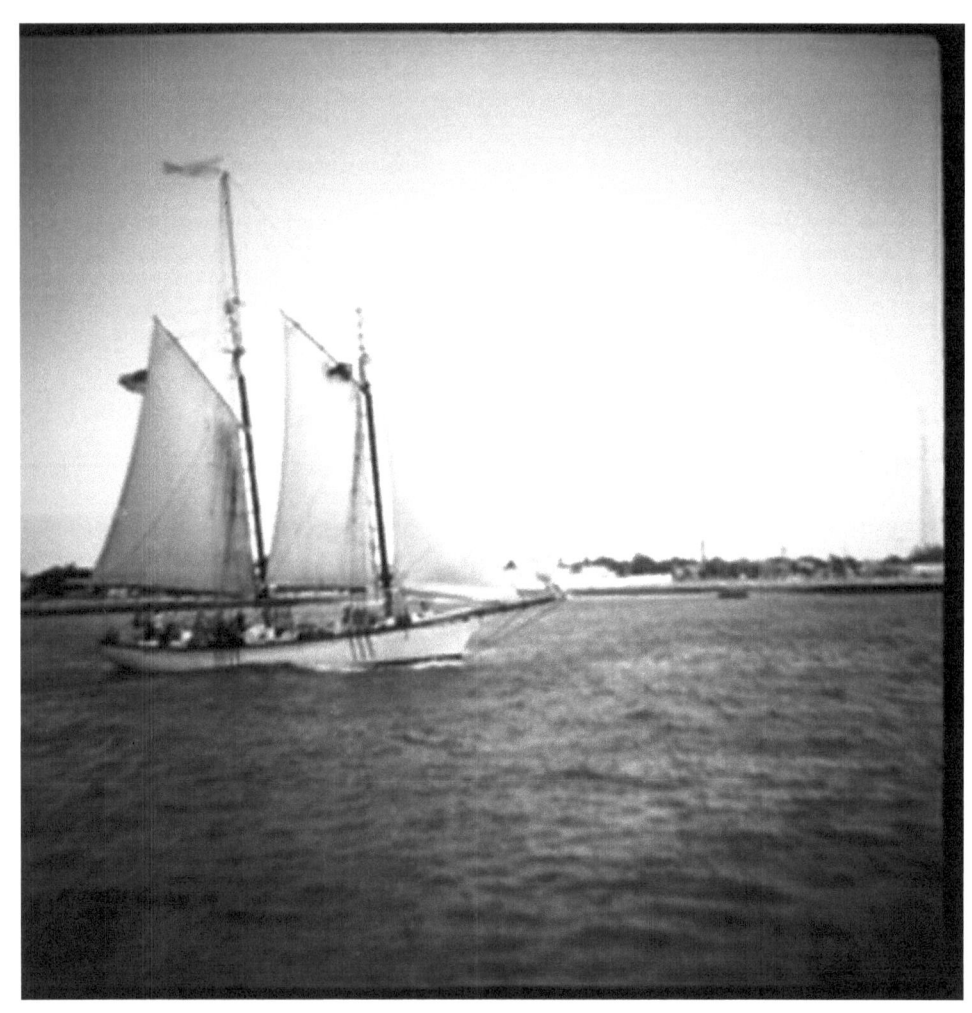

SCHOONER APPLEDORE

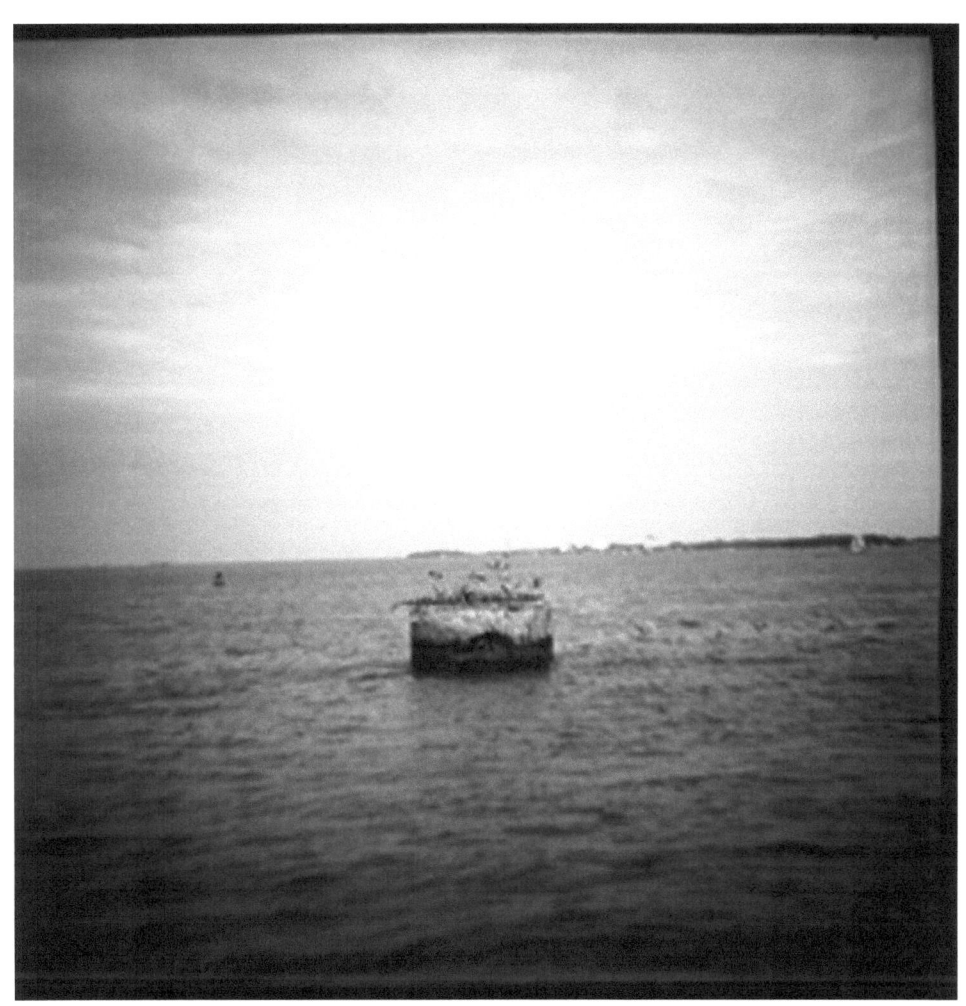

BIRD LANDING

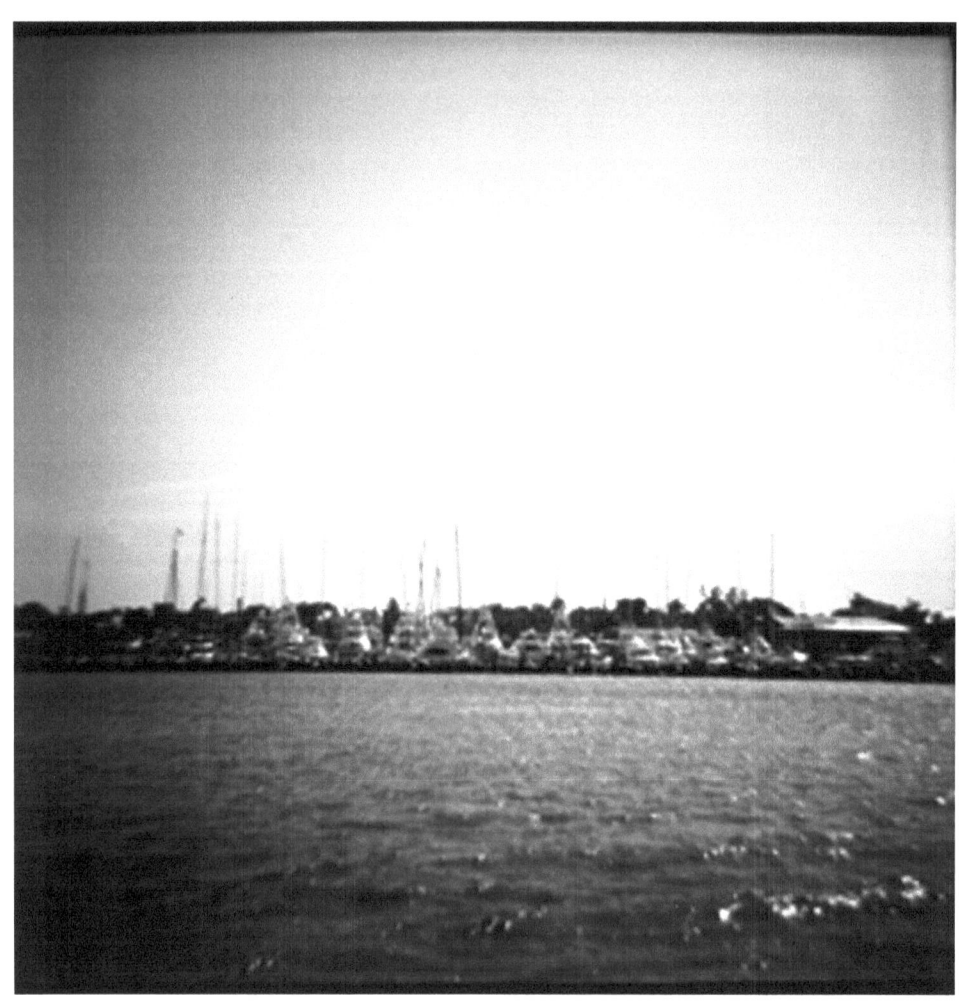

HARBOR

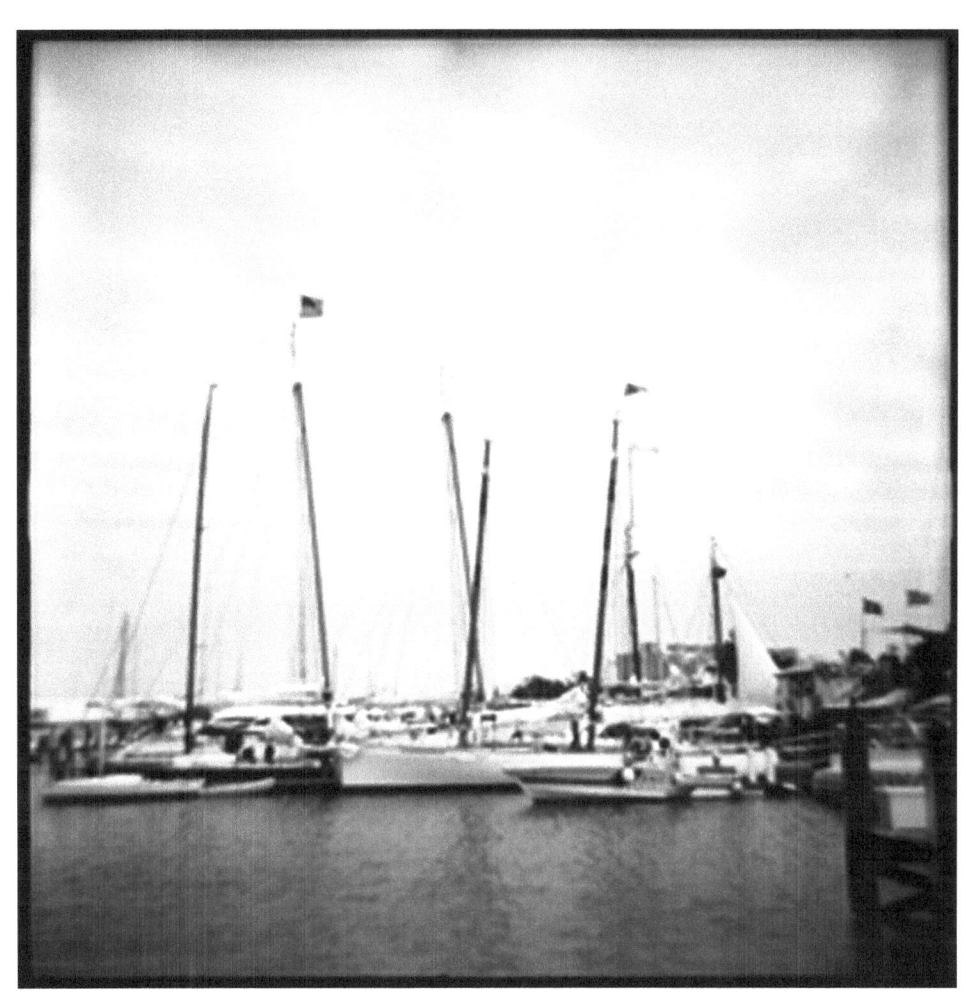

SAILBOATS

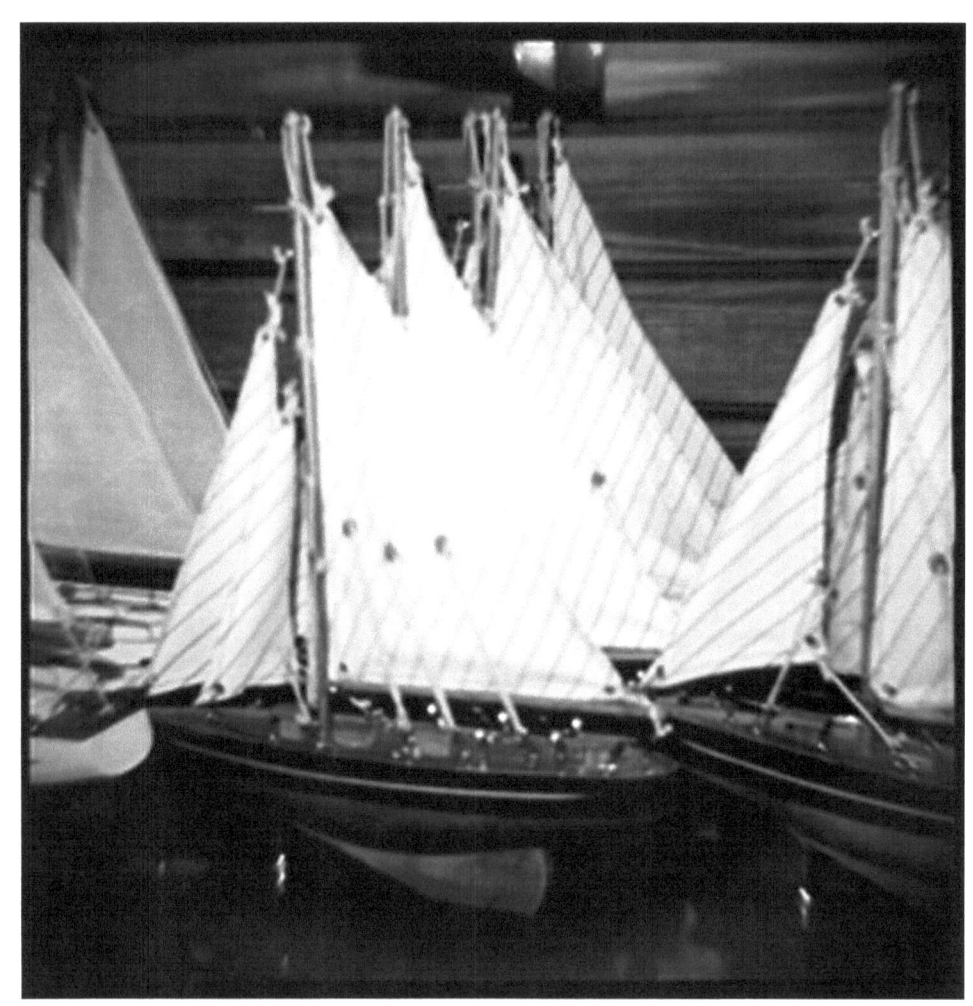

TOY SAILBOATS

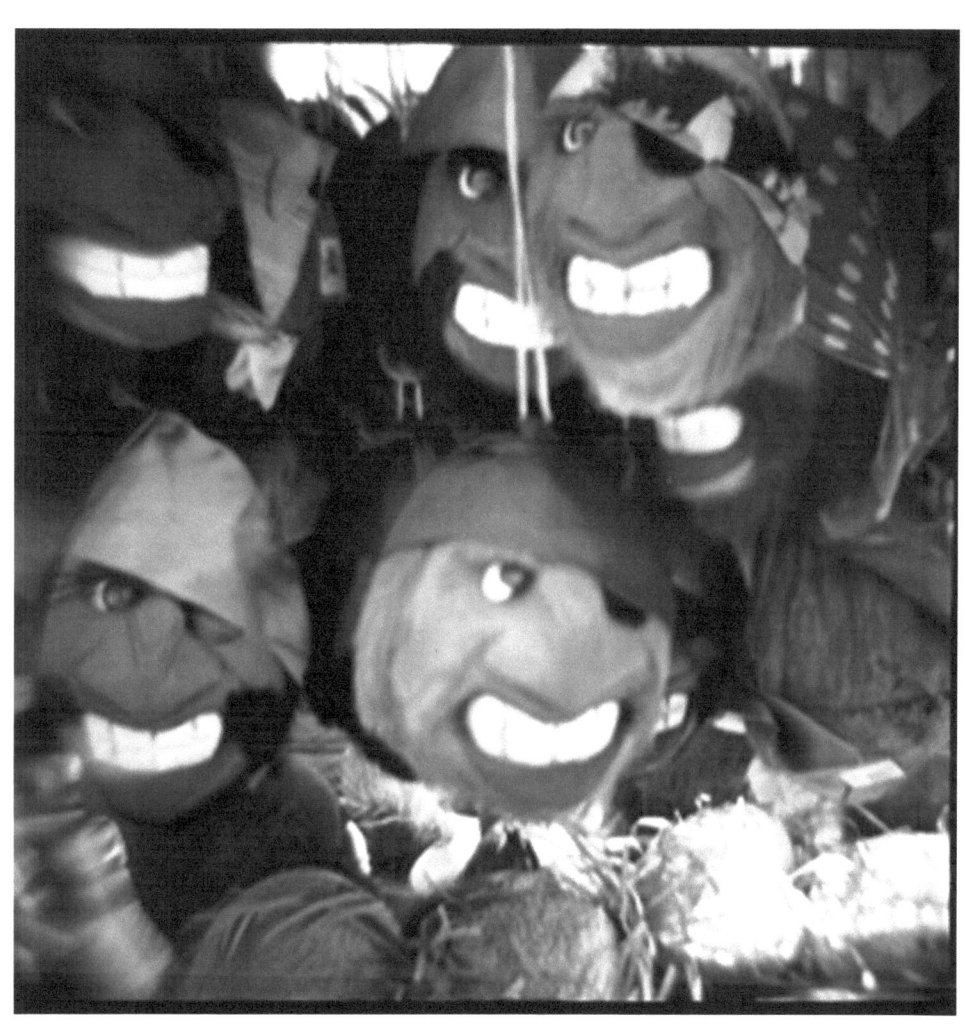

PIRATE HEADS

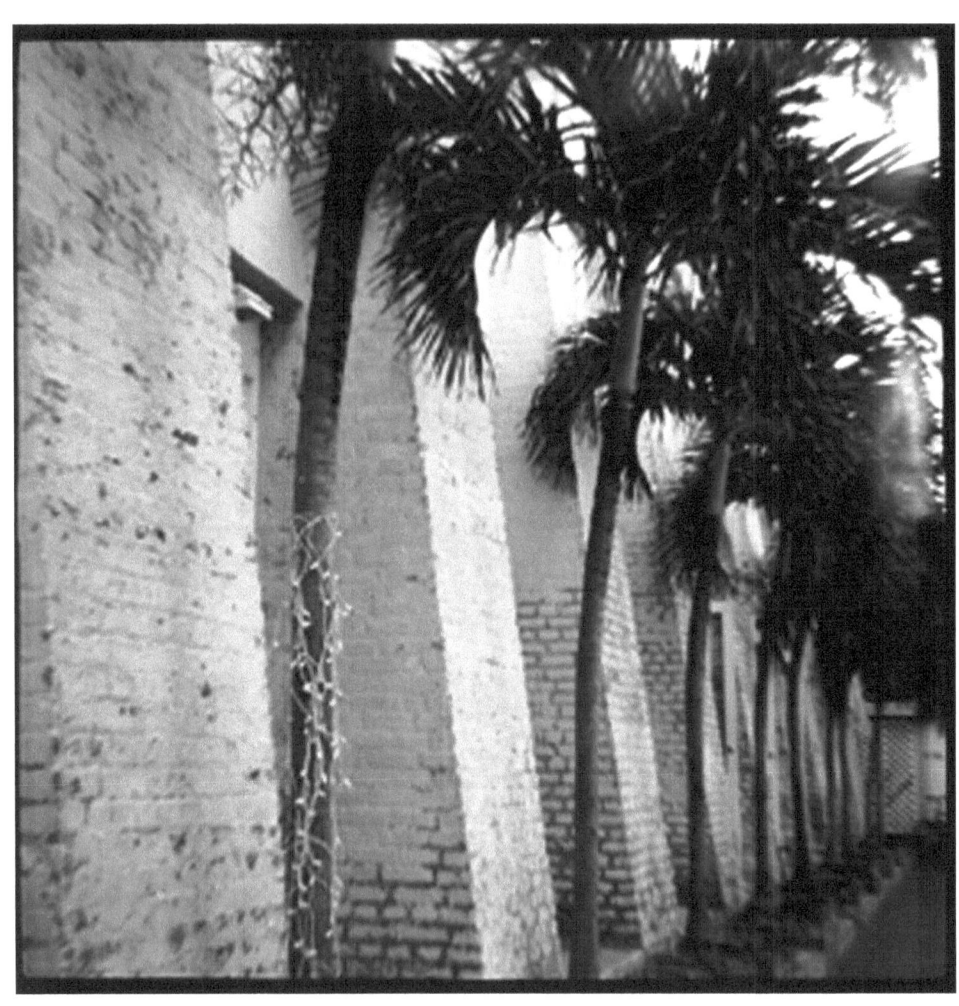

ROW OF PALMS

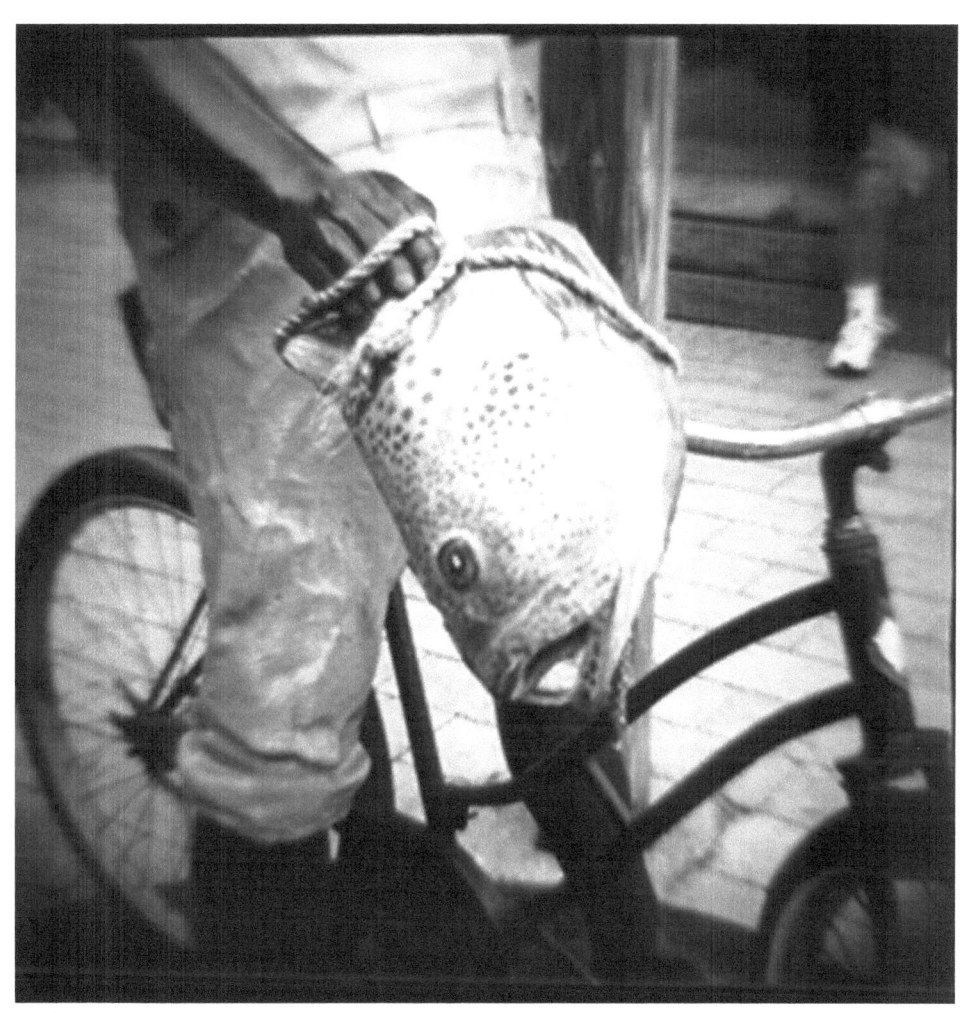

FISH HEAD

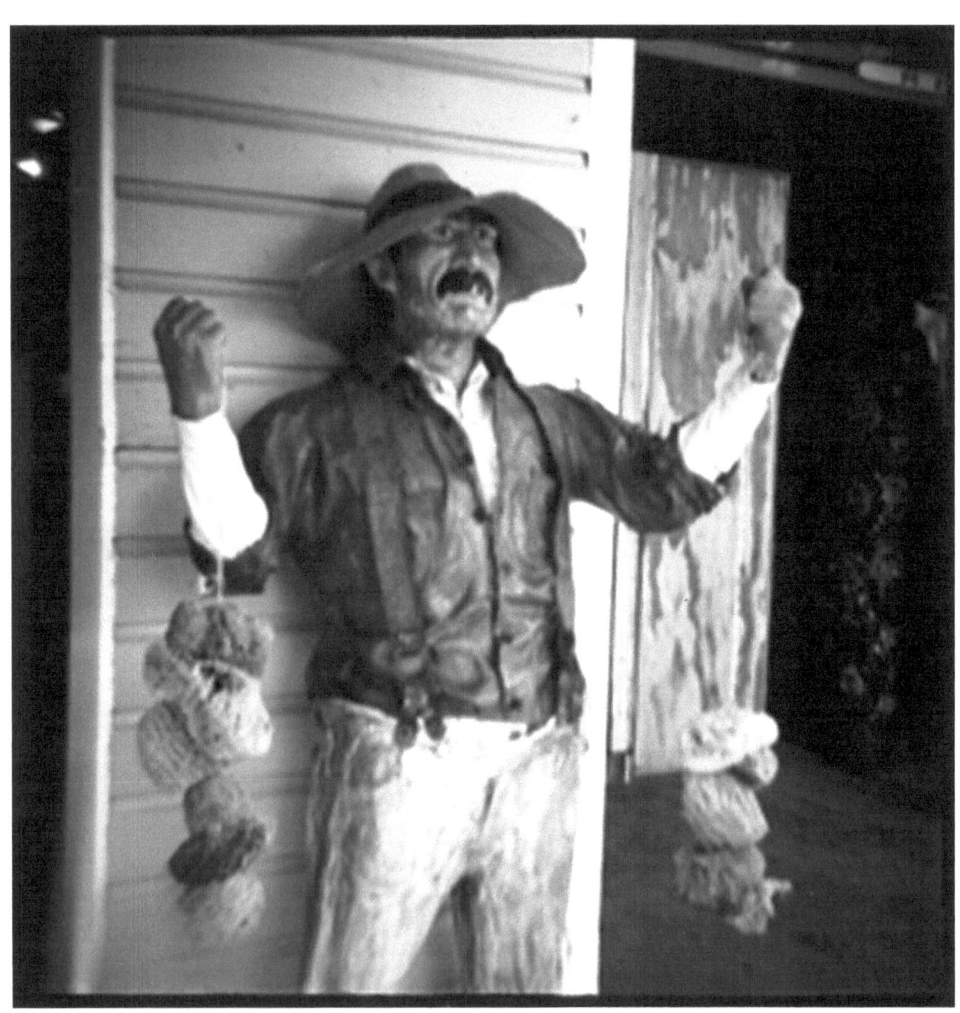

SPONGE SELLER

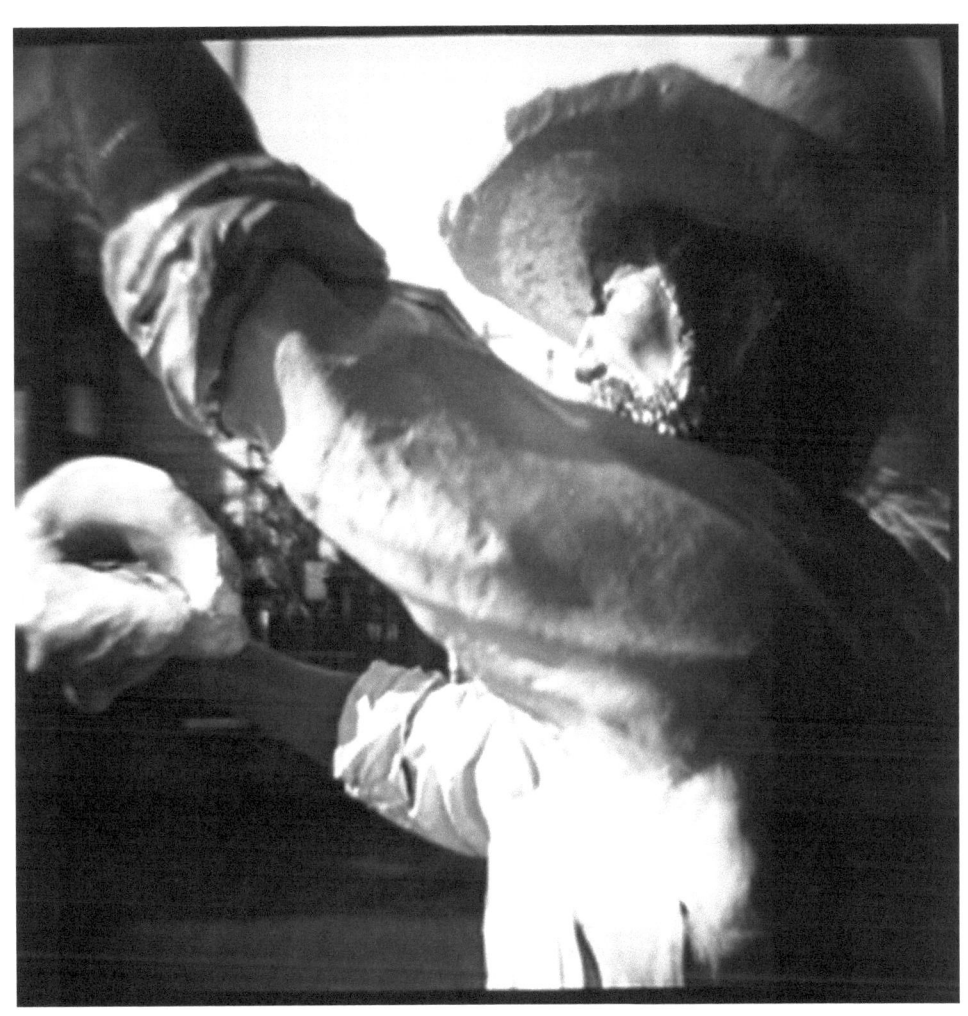

CONCH SELLER

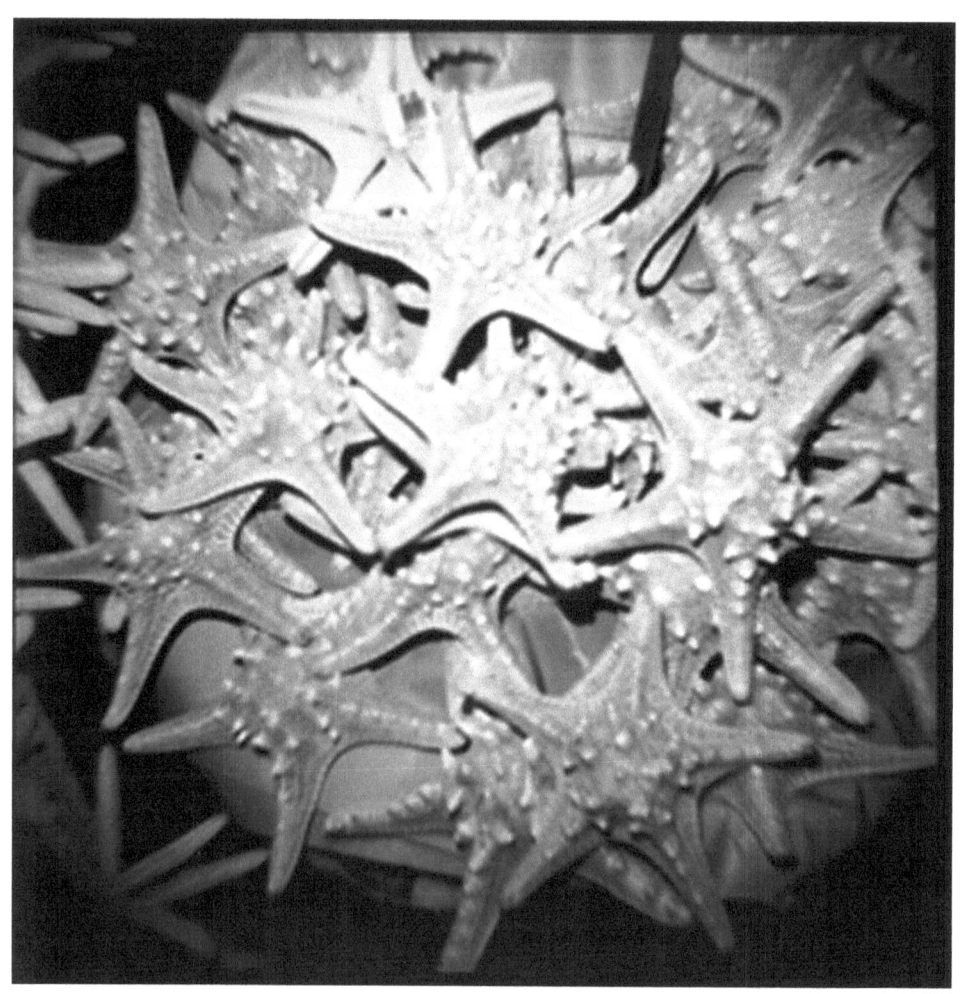

STARFISH

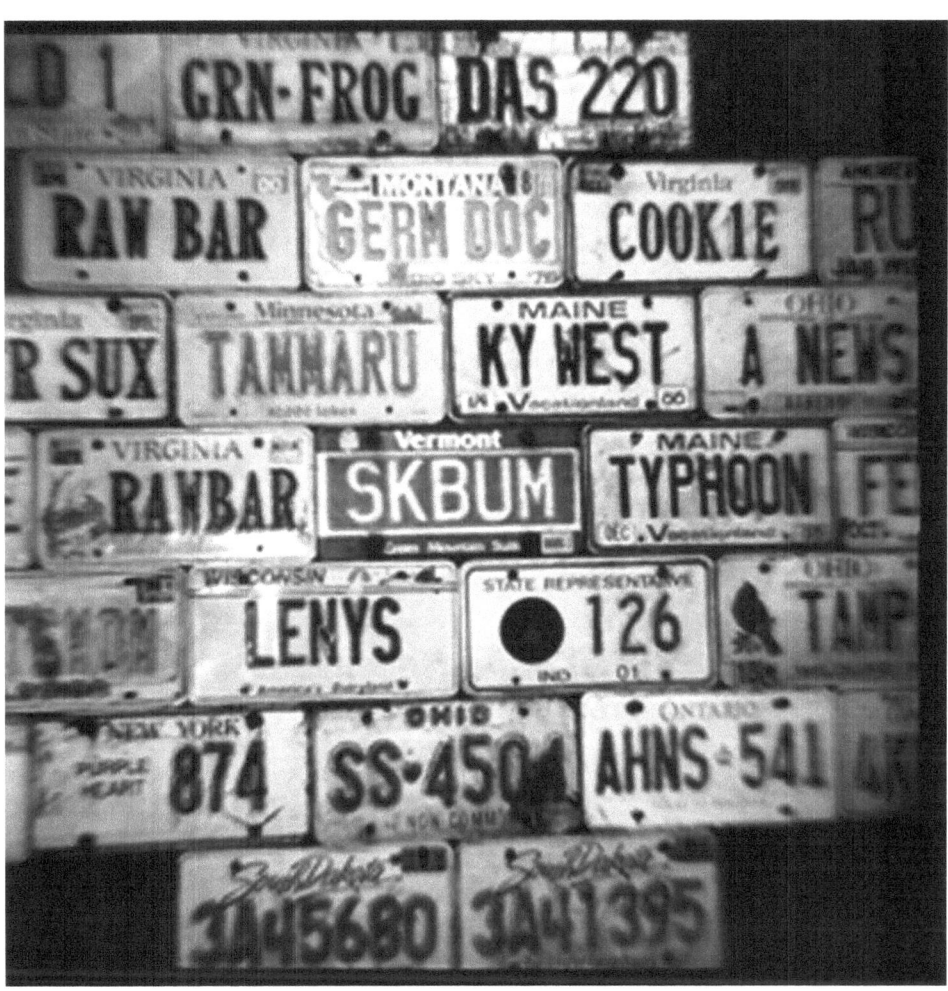

LICENSE PLATES
Half Shell Raw Bar

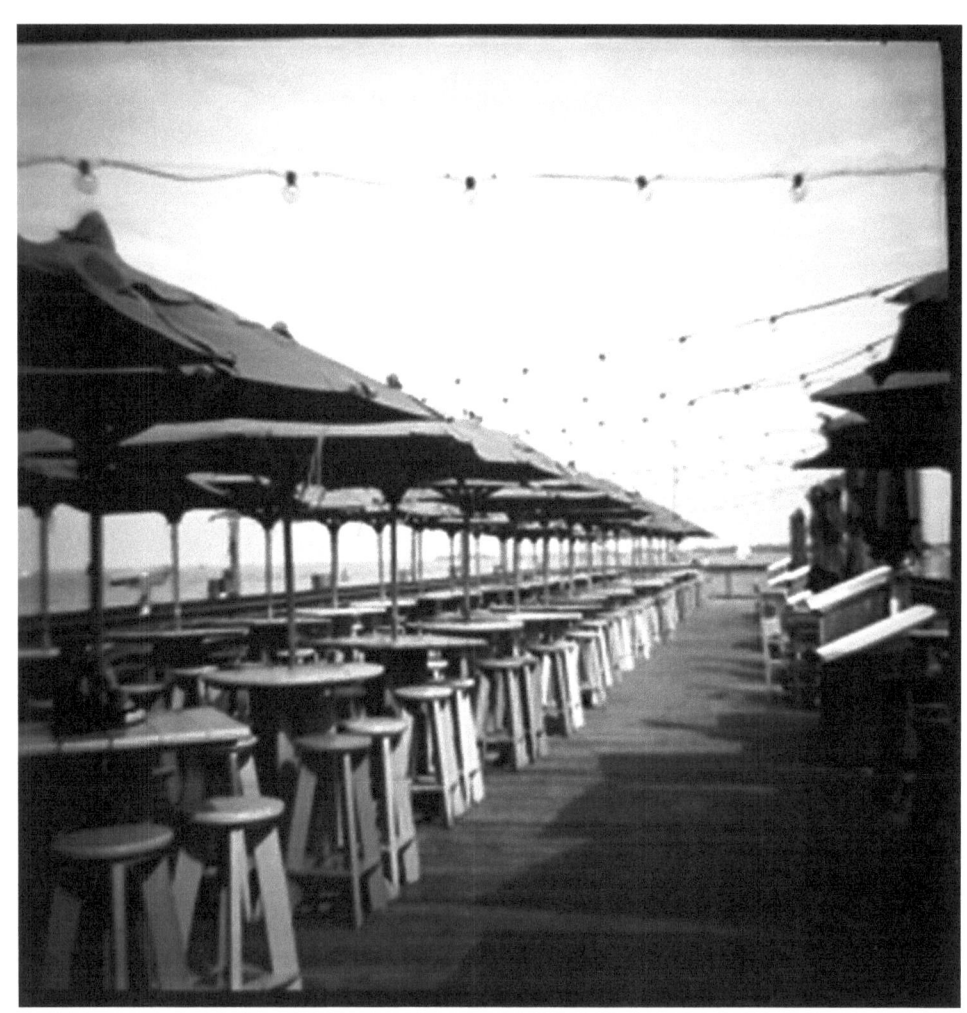

SUNSET PIER

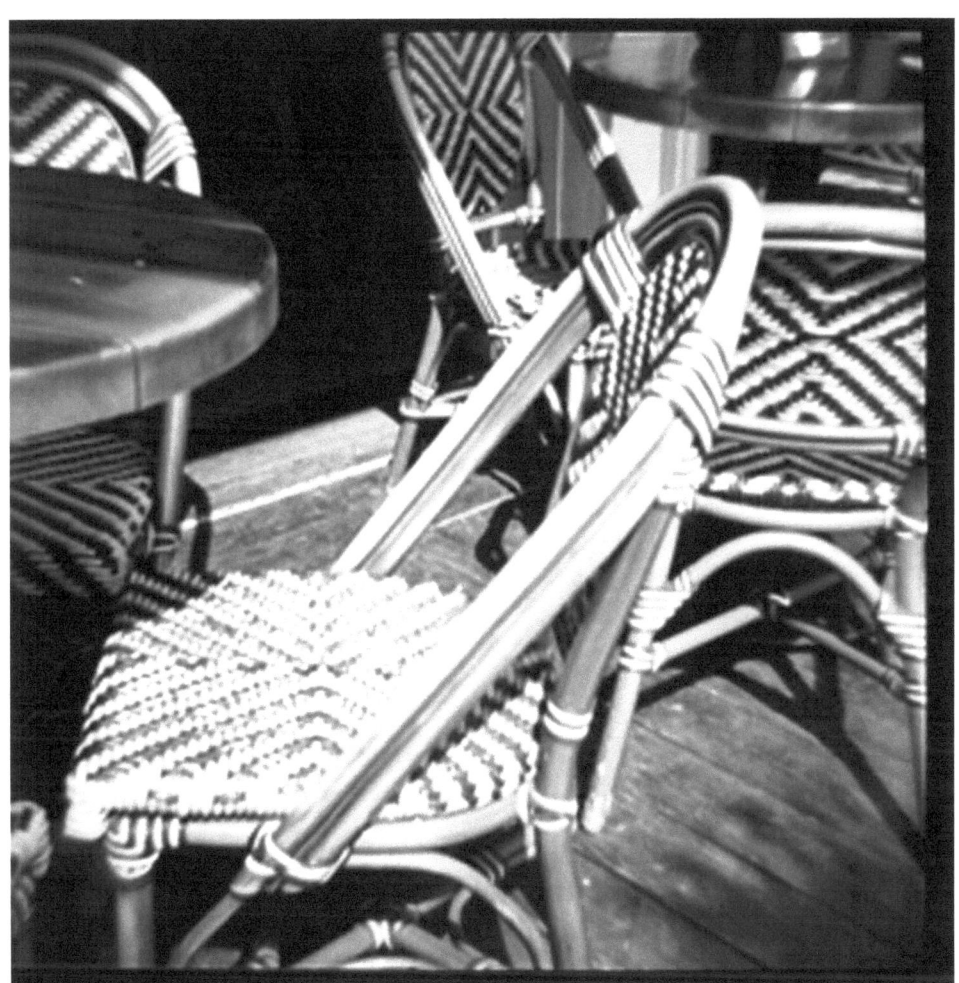

RATTAN CHAIRS

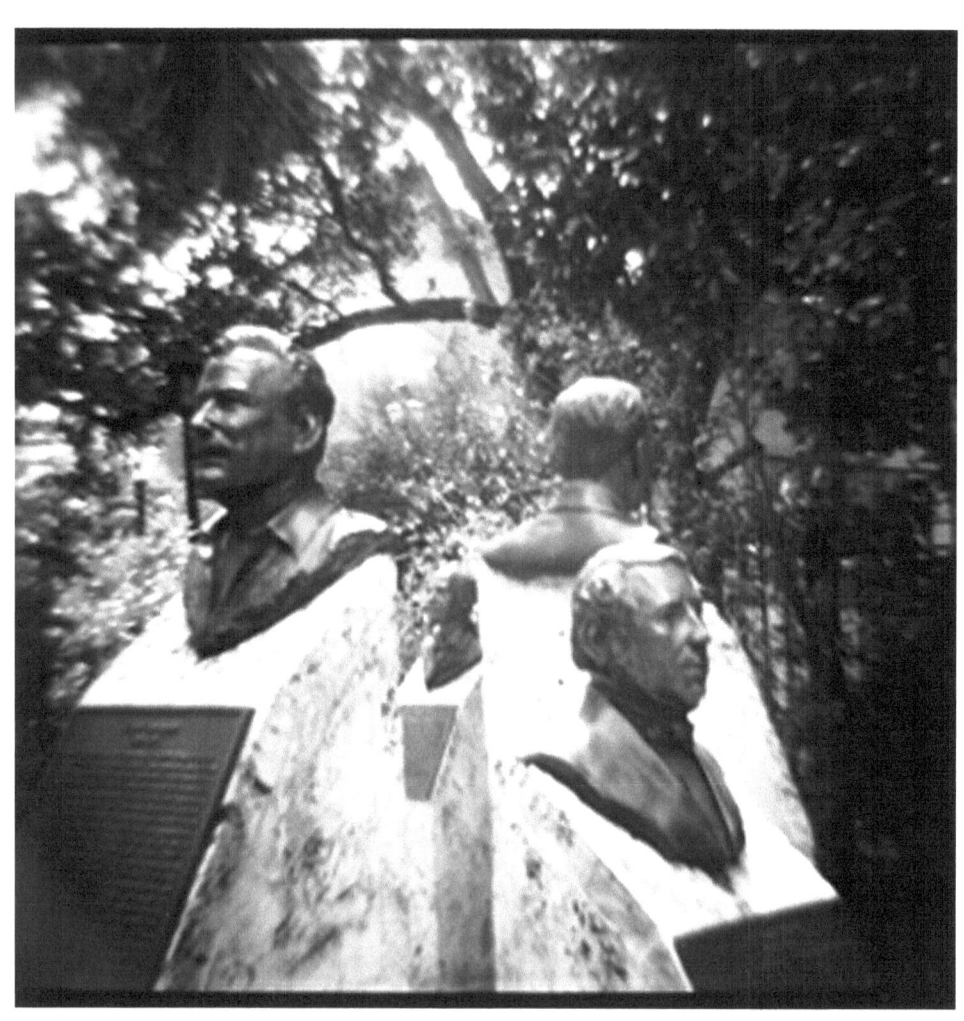

SCULPTURE PARK ONE

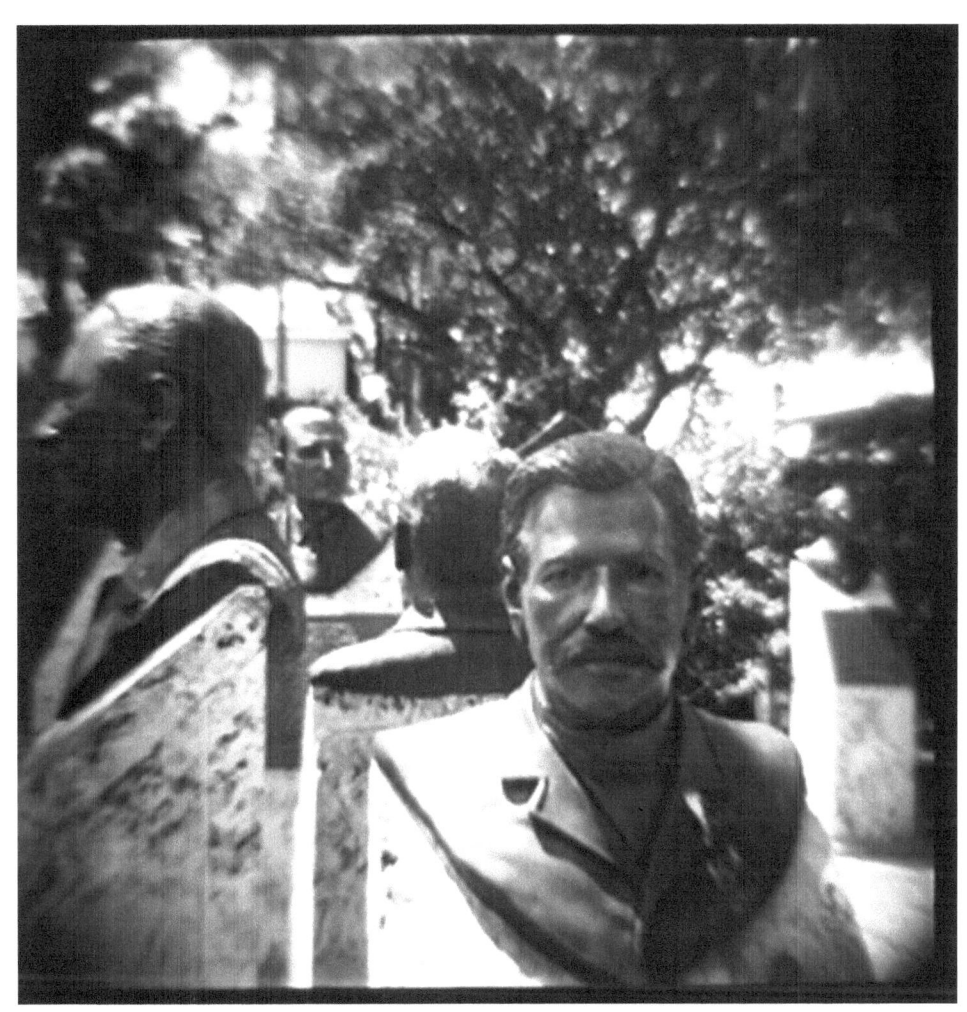

SCULPTURE PARK TWO

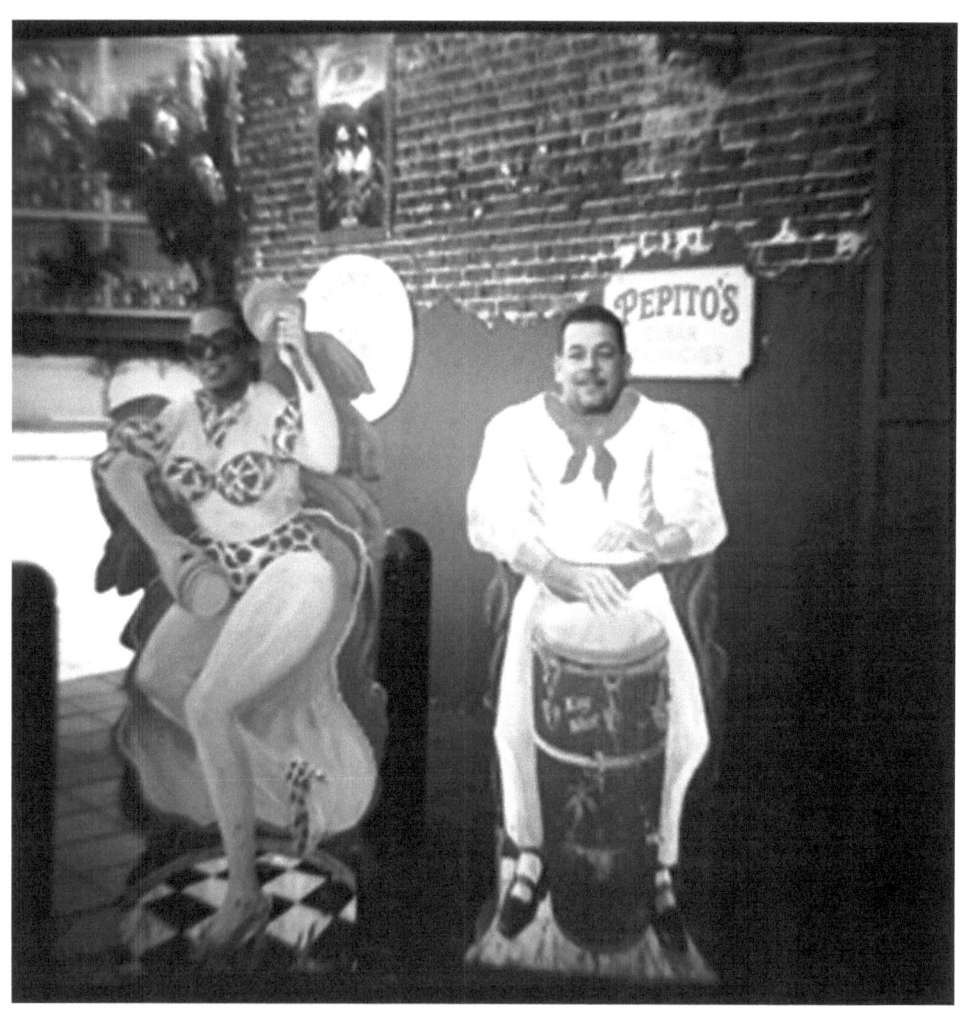

CUBAN CUTOUTS

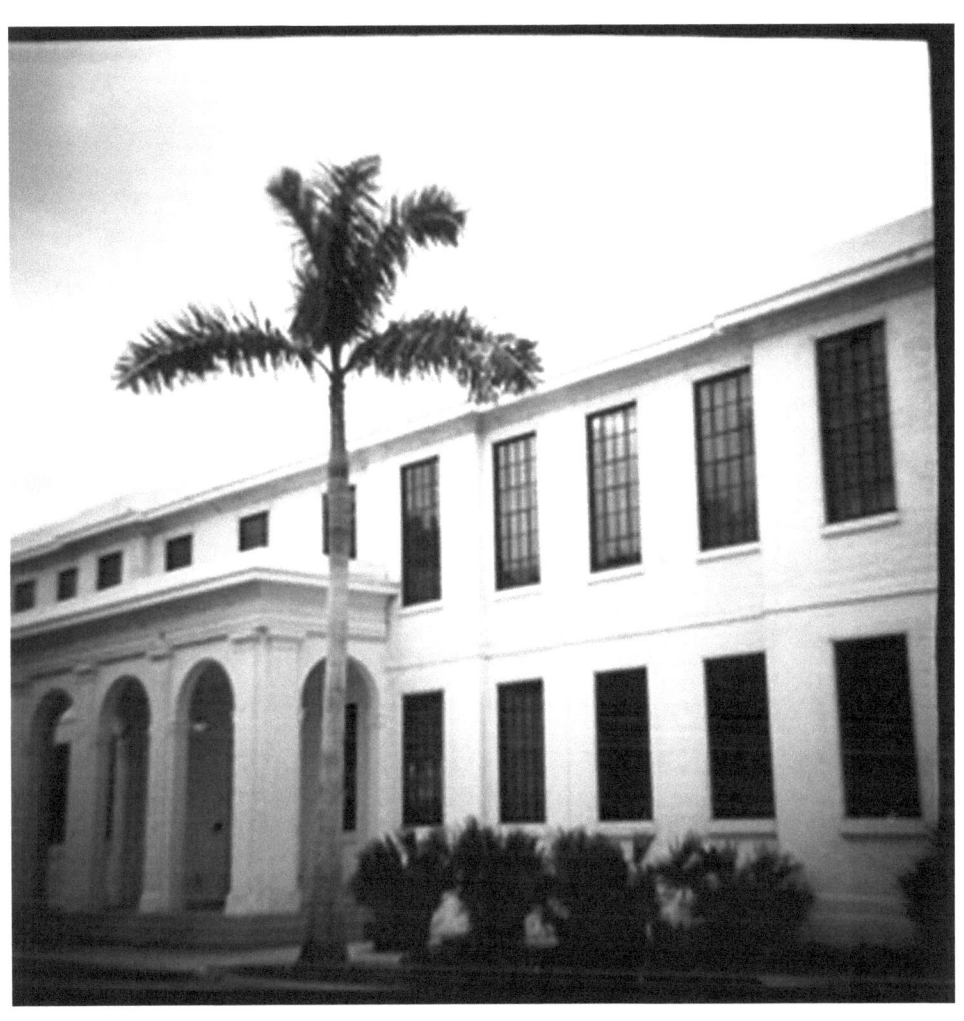

GATO BUILDING
Early Cigar Factory

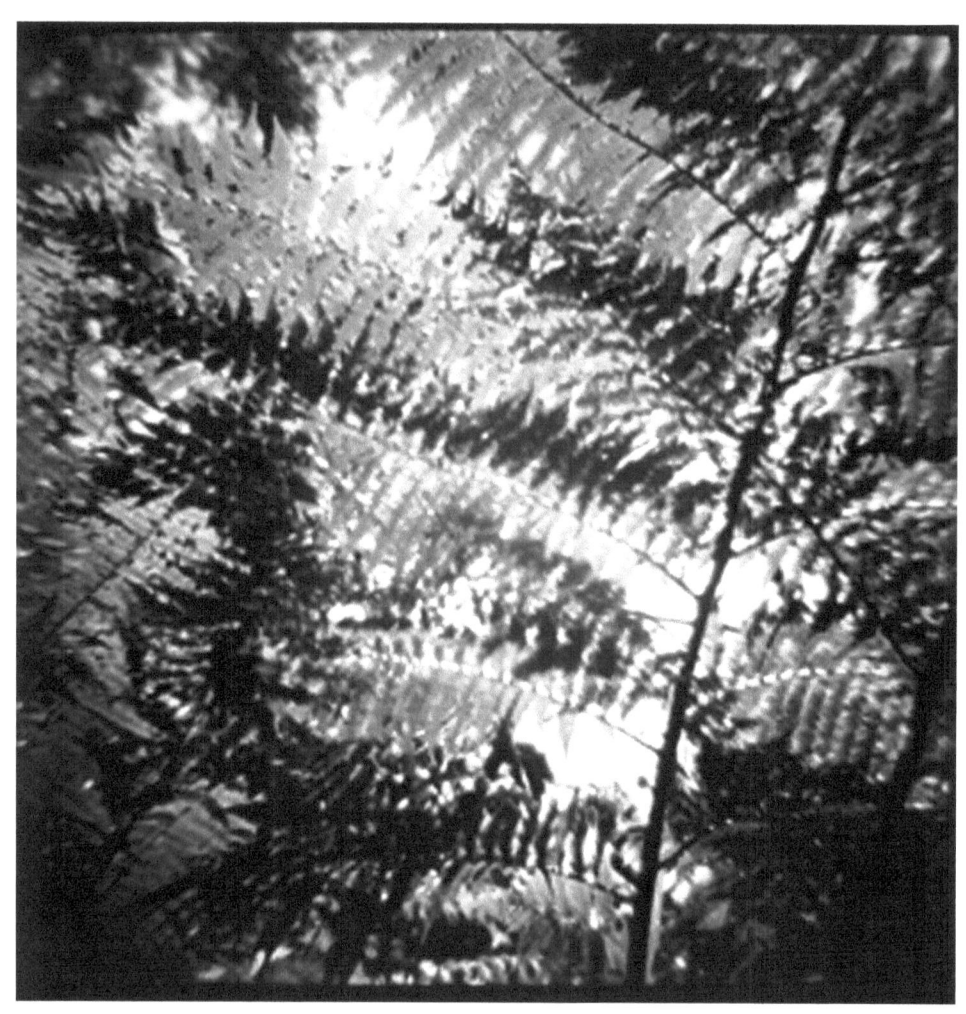

FERNS
NANCY FORESTER'S SECRET GARDEN

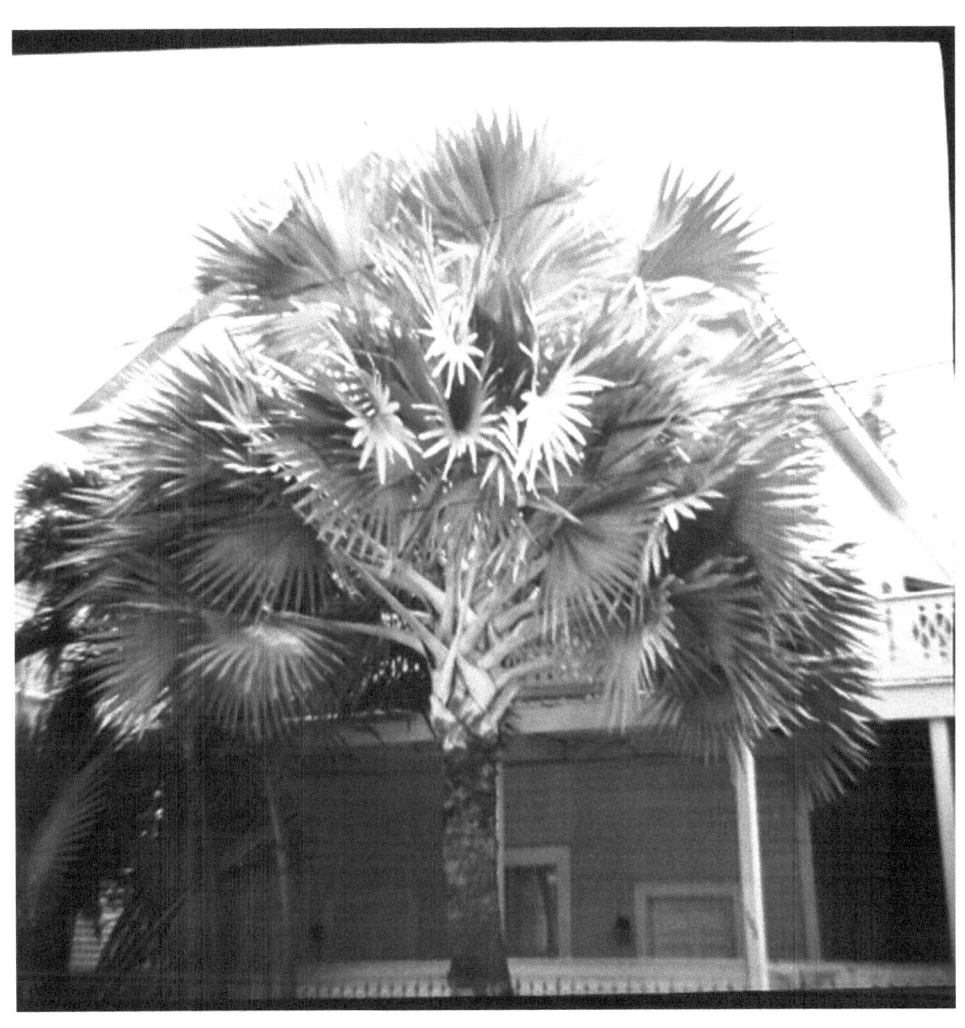

PALMETTO TREE

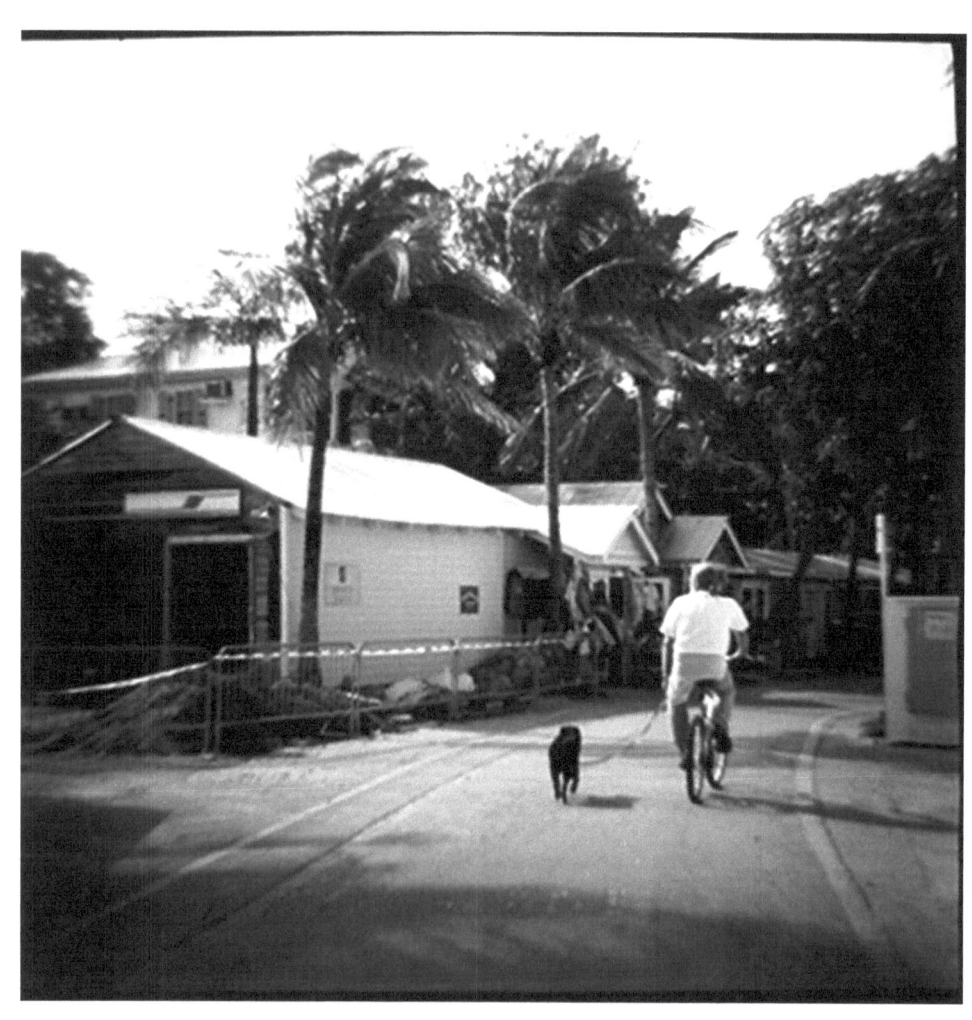

BICYCLE RIDER WITH DOG

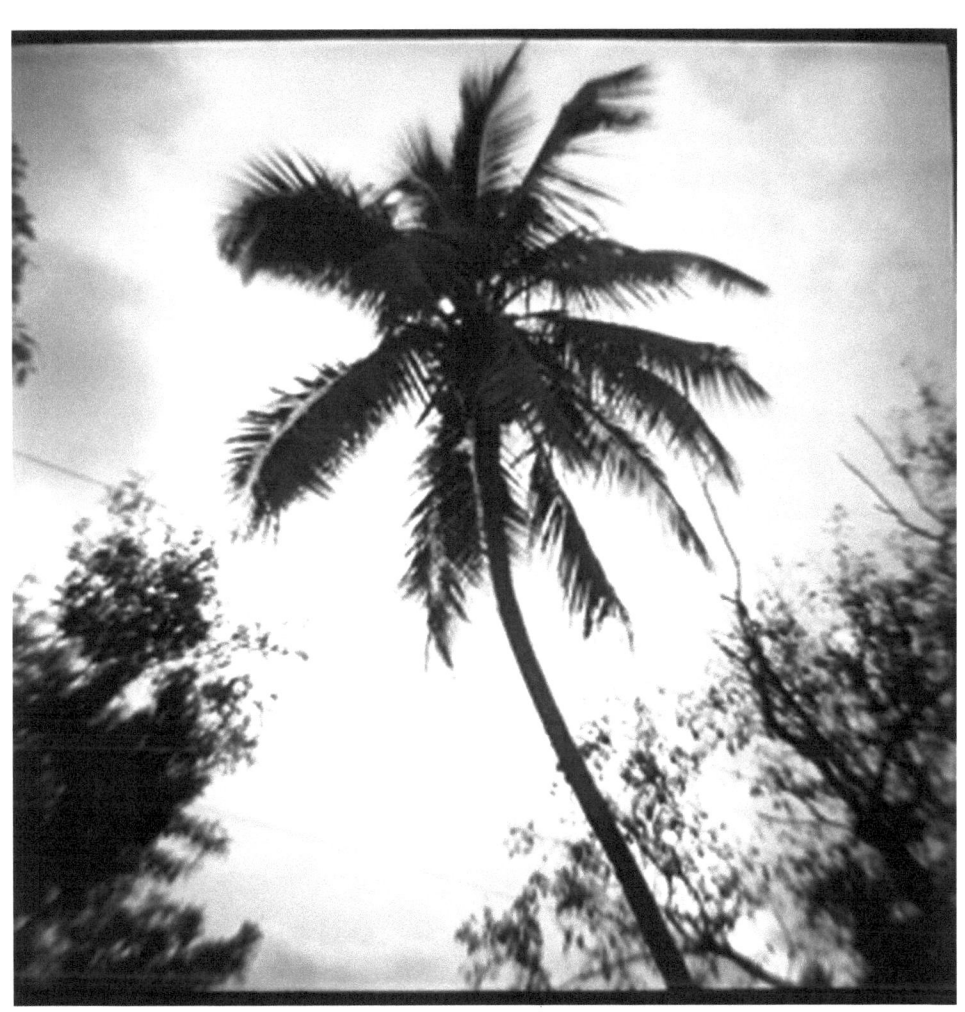

SOLITARY PALM

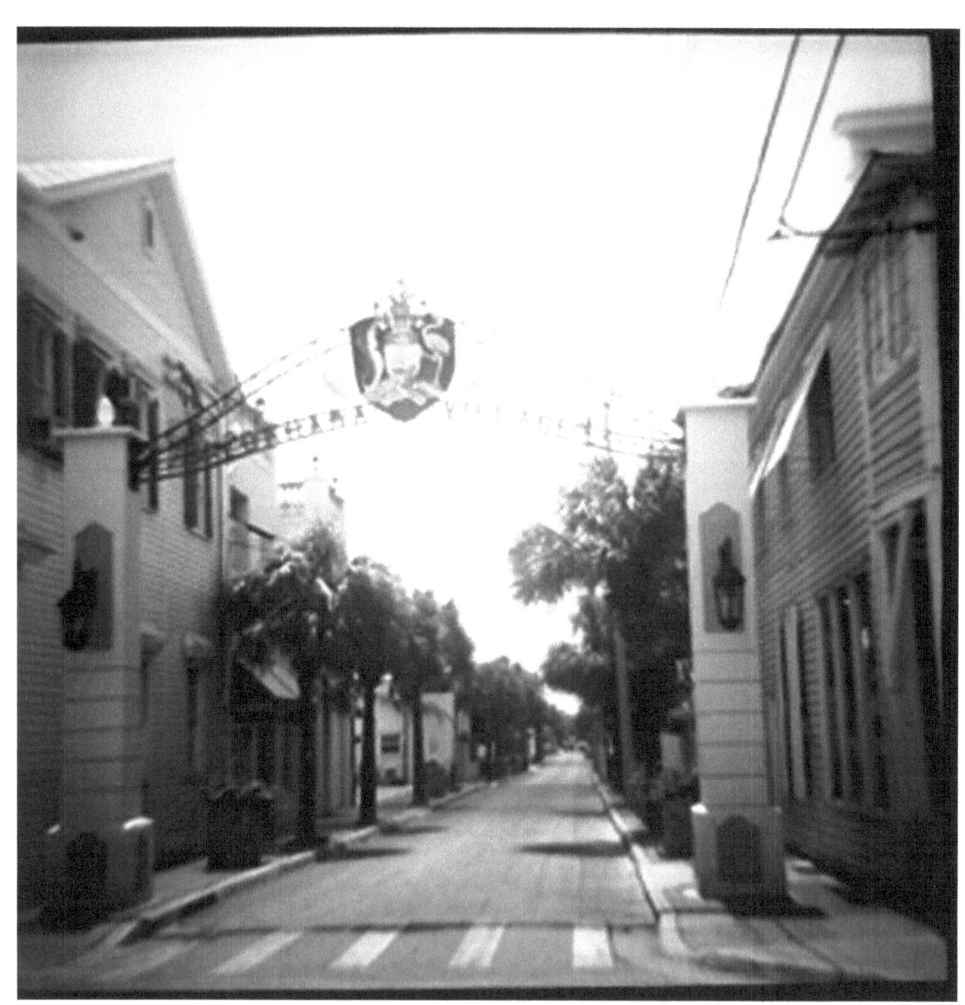

BAHAMA VILLAGE

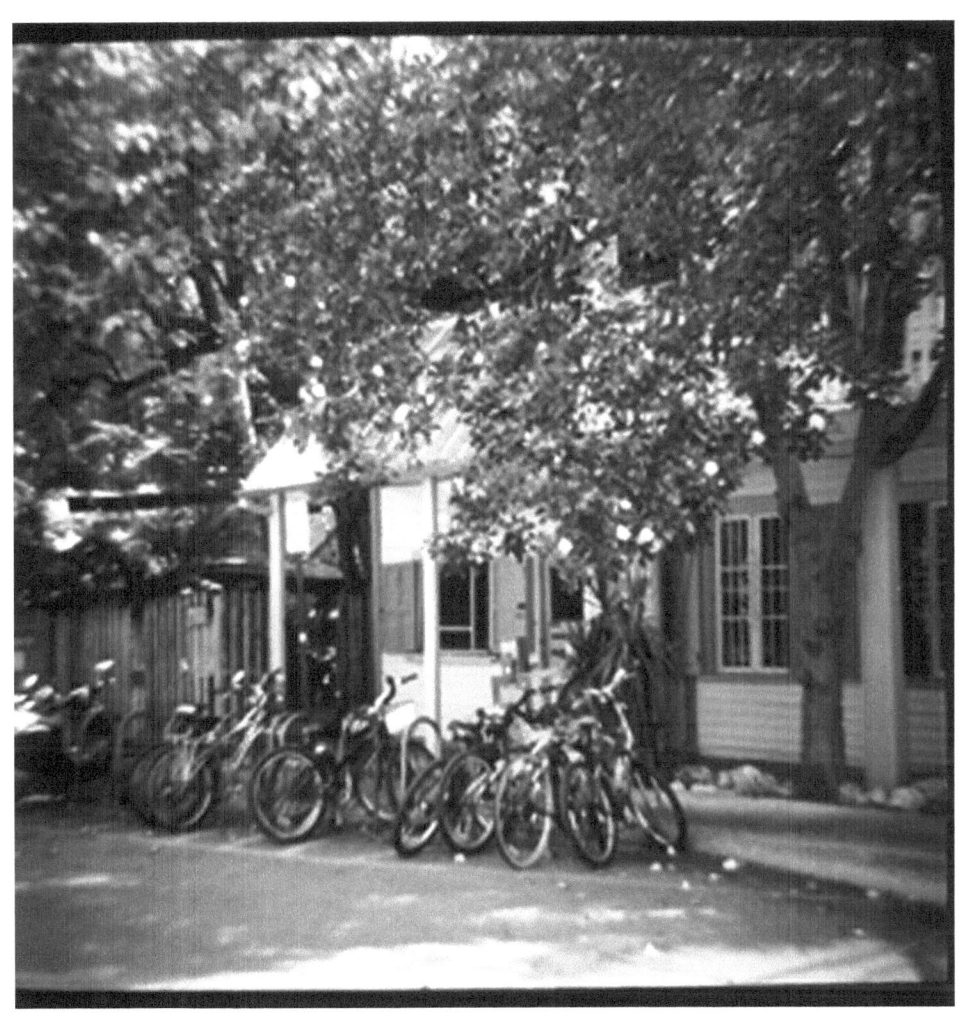

BLUE HEAVEN

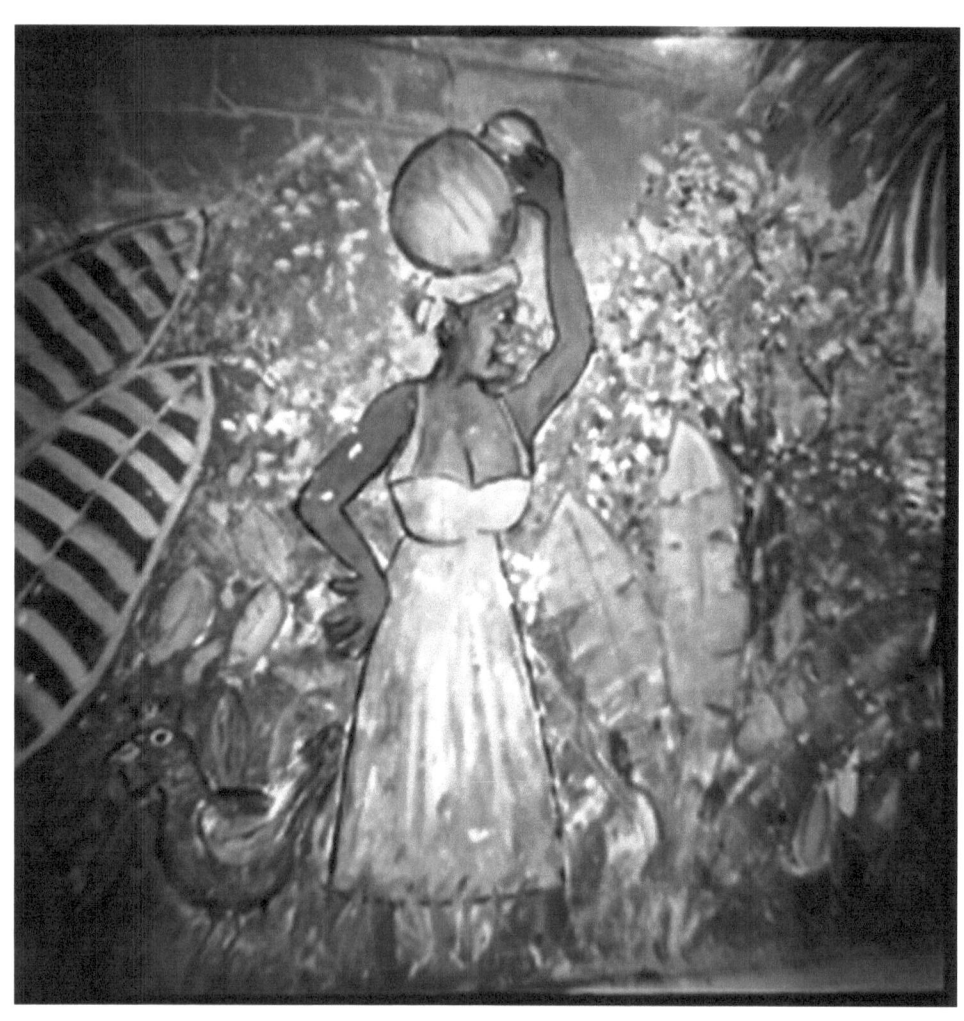

MURAL
BAHAMA VILLAGE

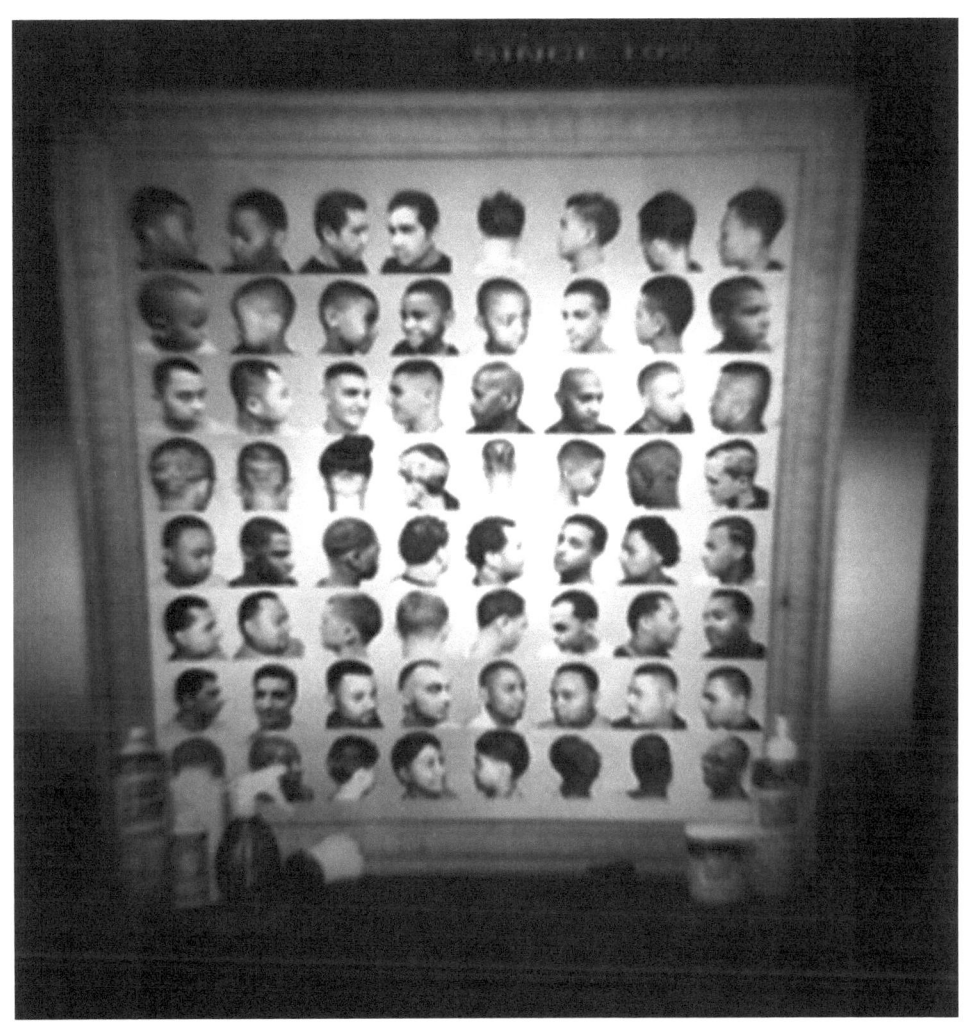

BARBERSHOP WINDOW

DUVAL STREET

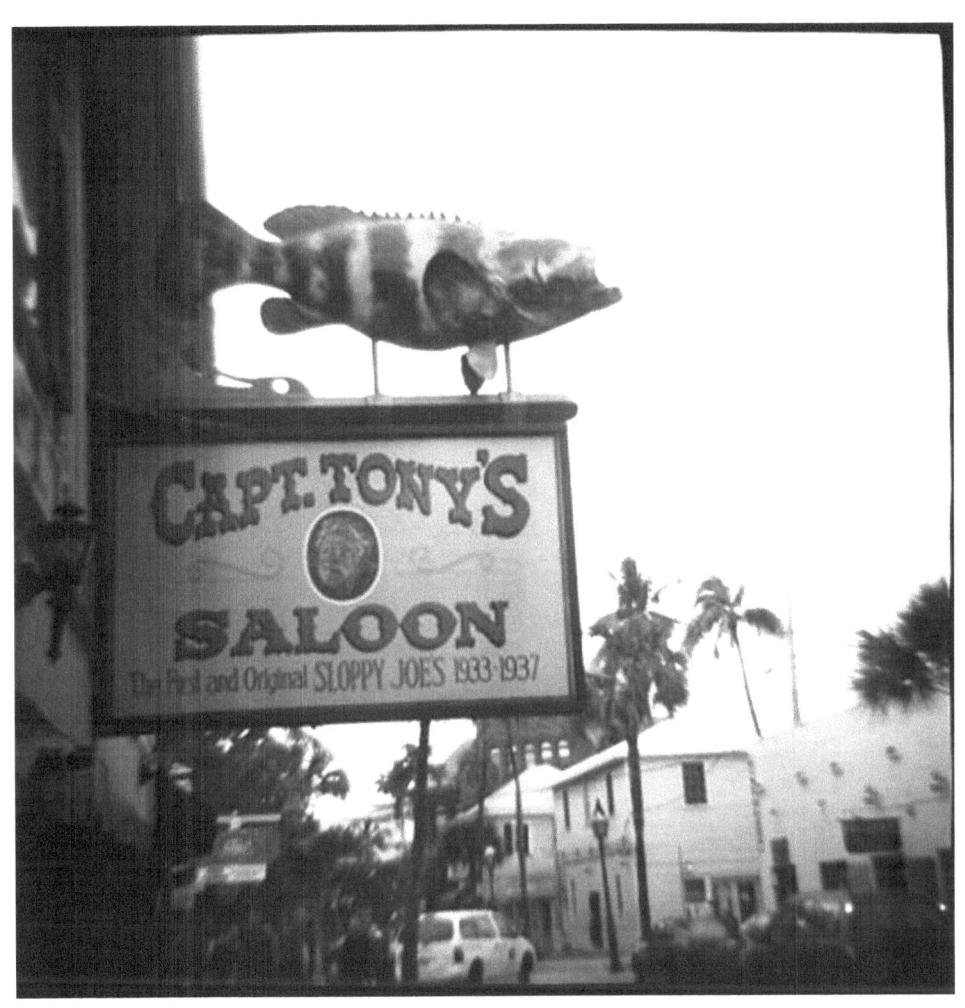

CAPT TONY'S SALOON

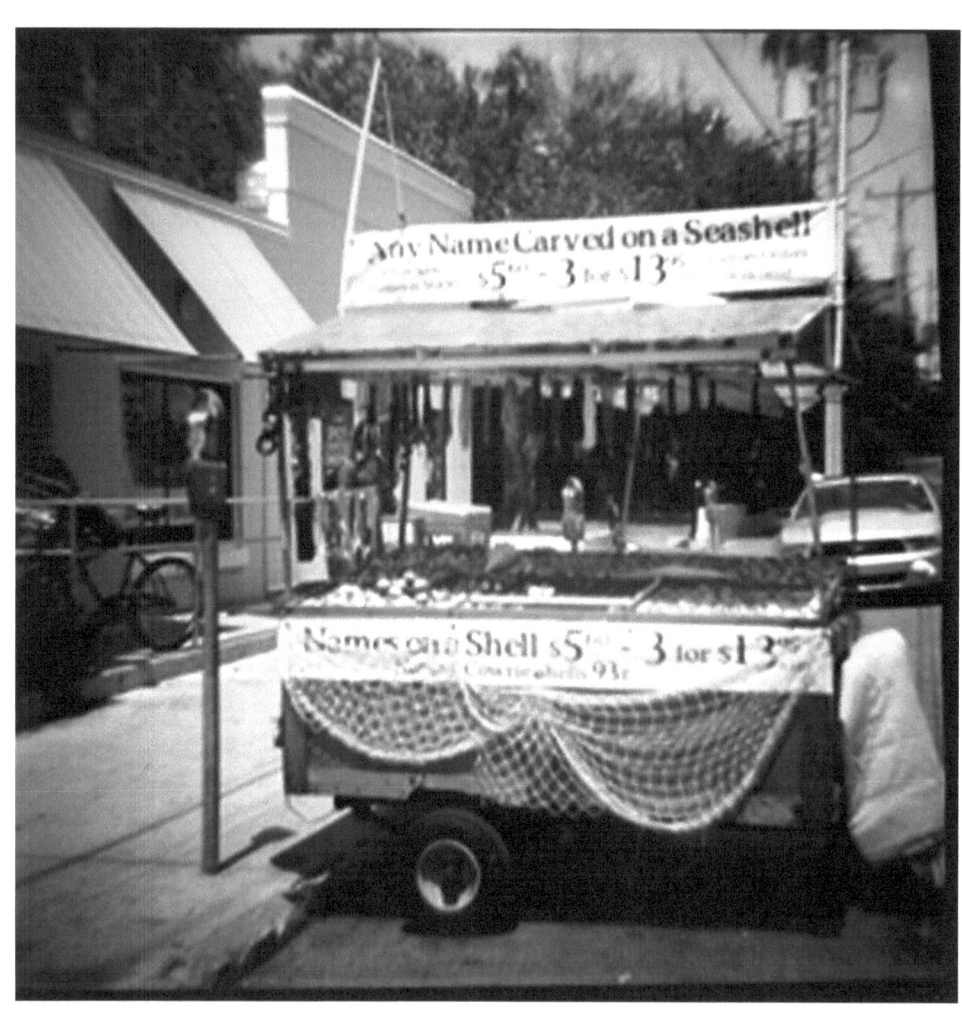

NAMES ON A SHELL

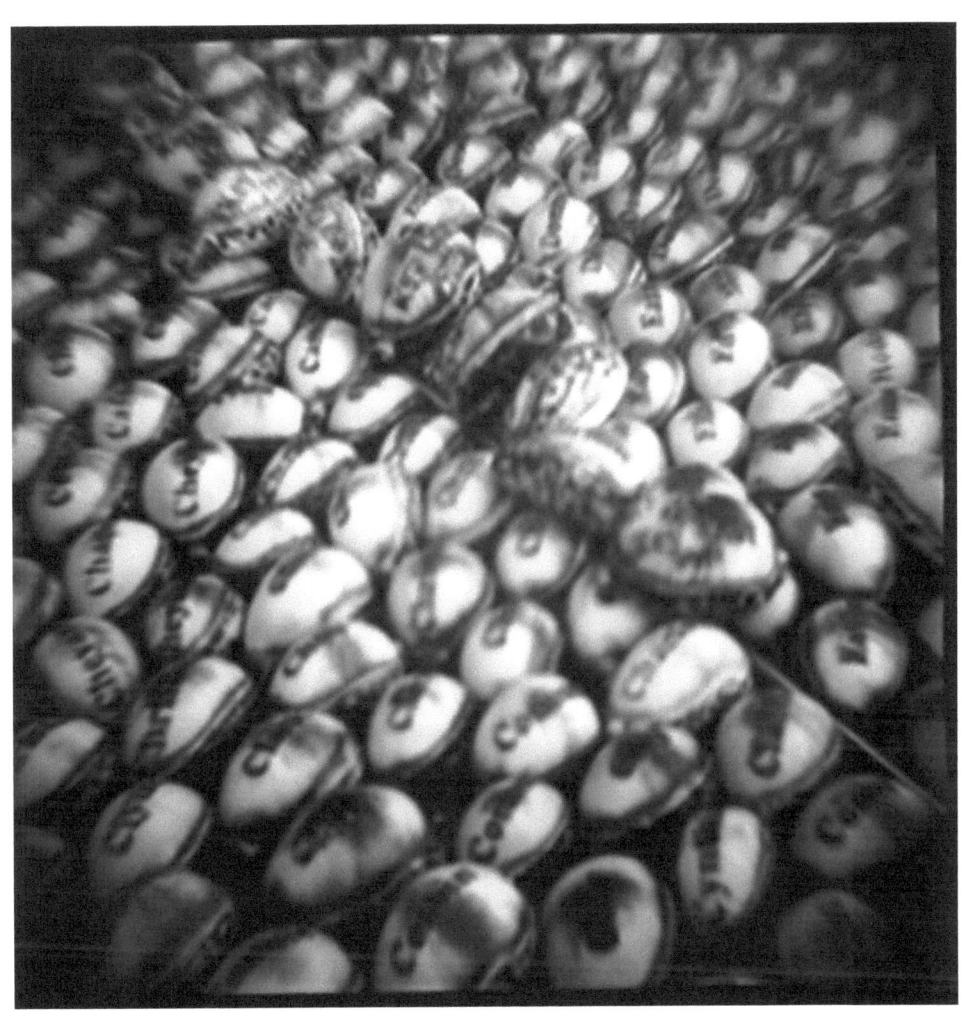

CARVED SHELLS

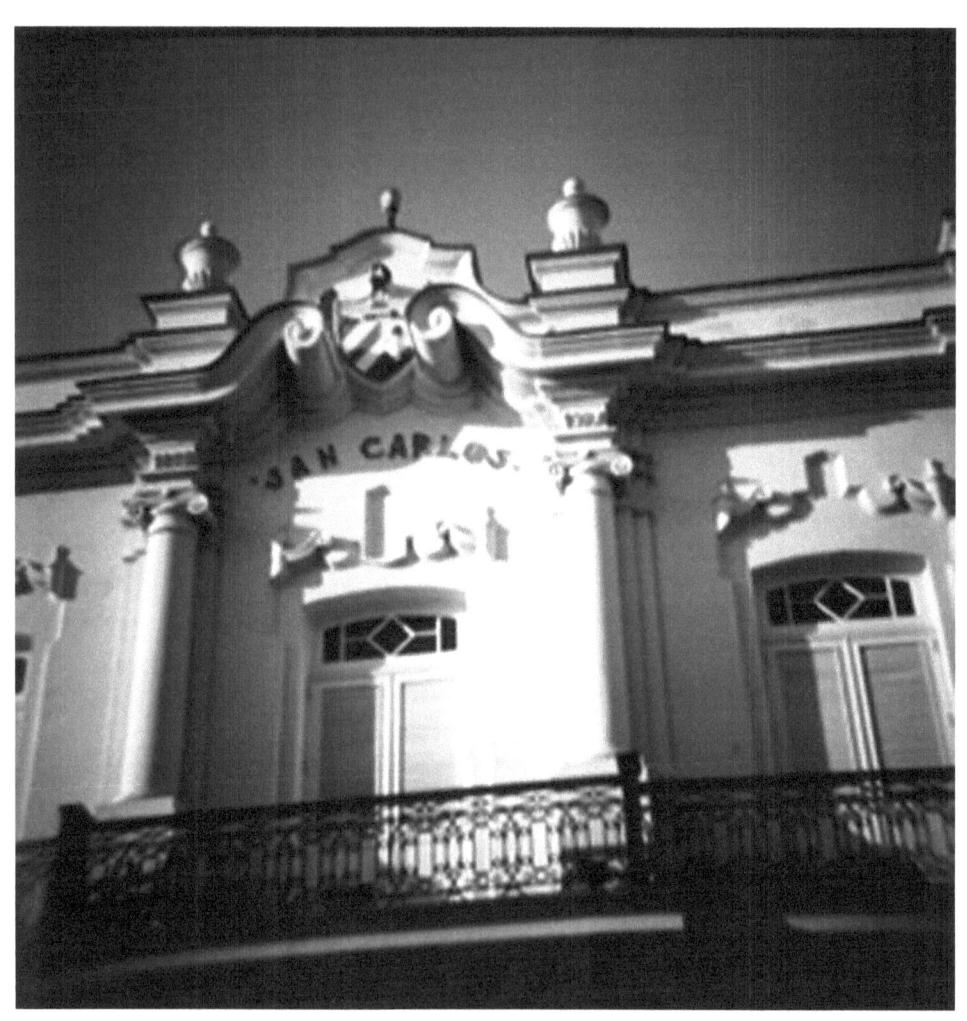

SAN CARLOS INSTITUTE

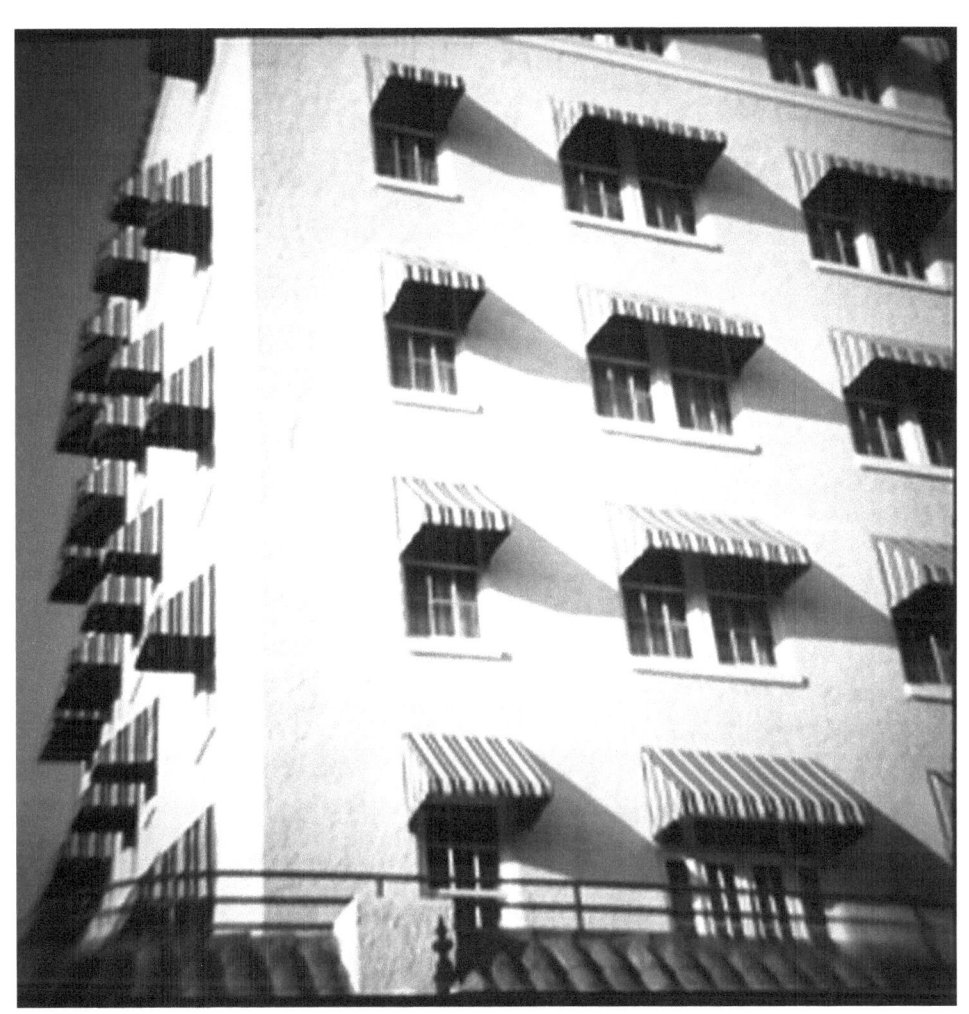

LA CONCHA HOTEL

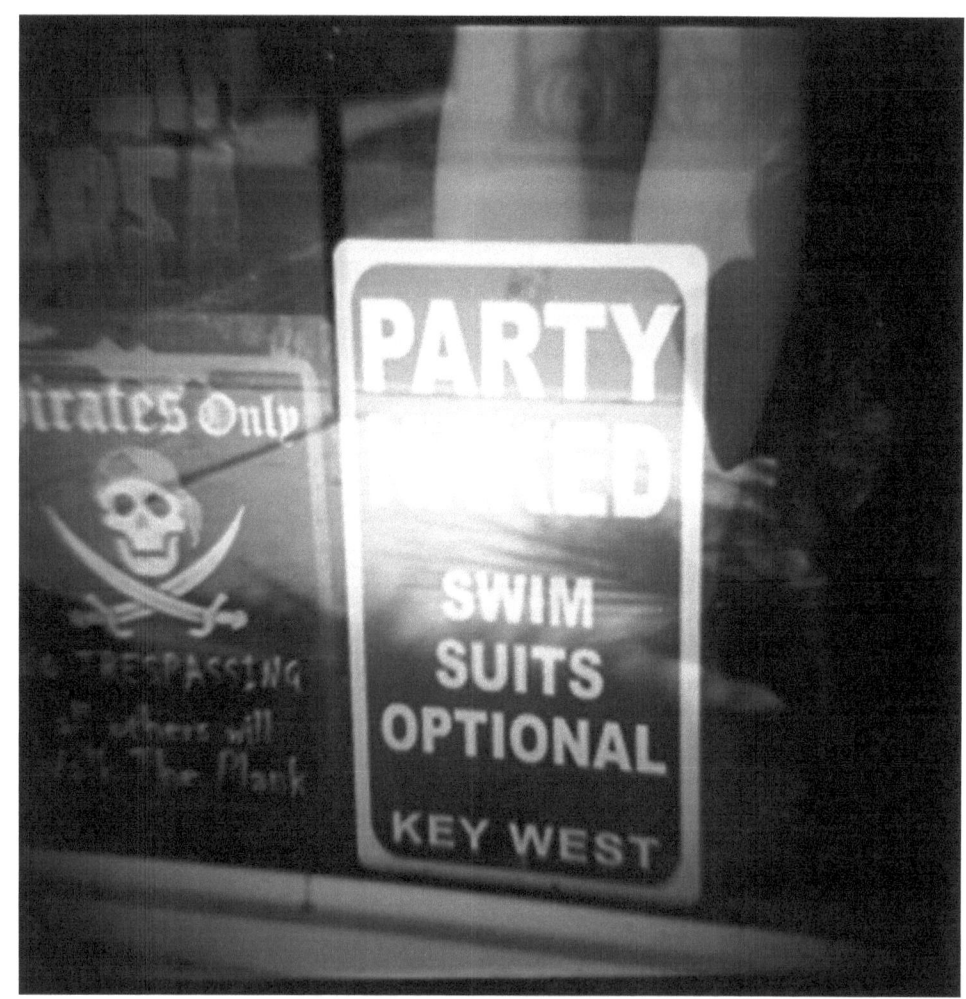

PARTY NAKED WINDOW

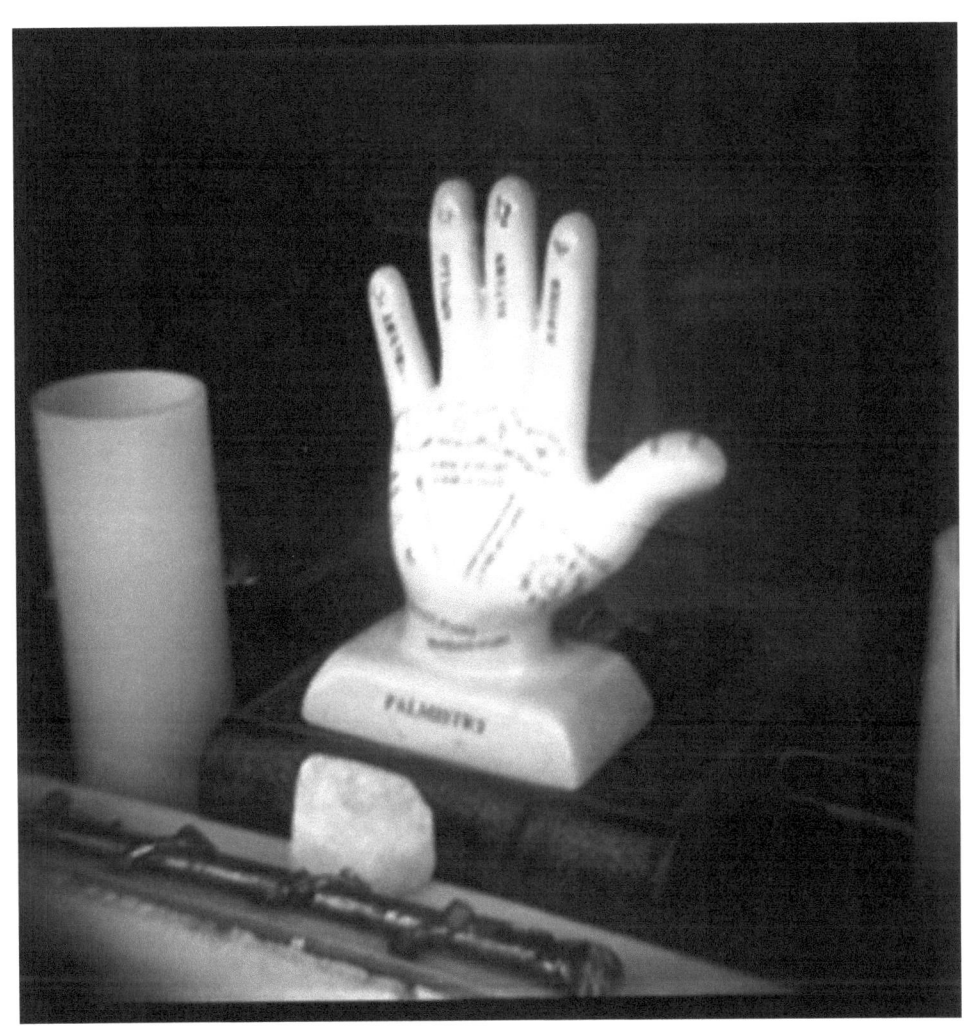

PALMISTRY WINDOW

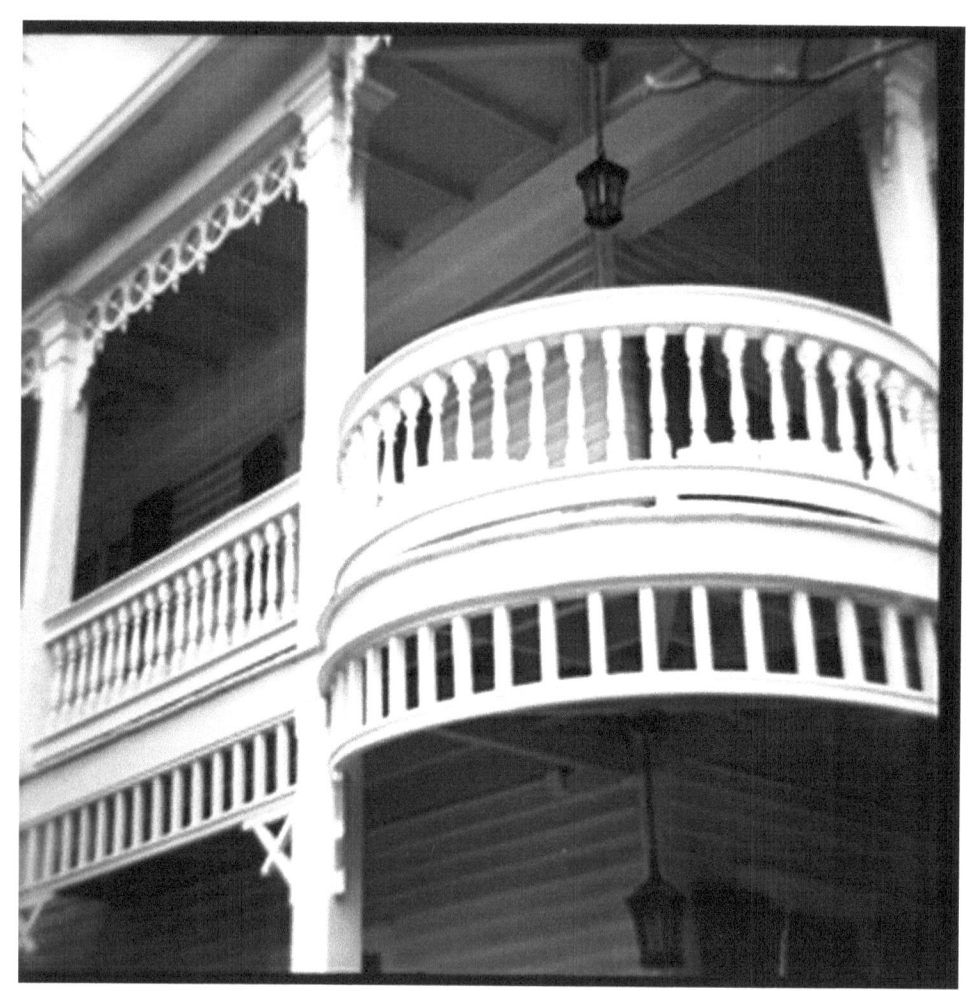

BALCONY

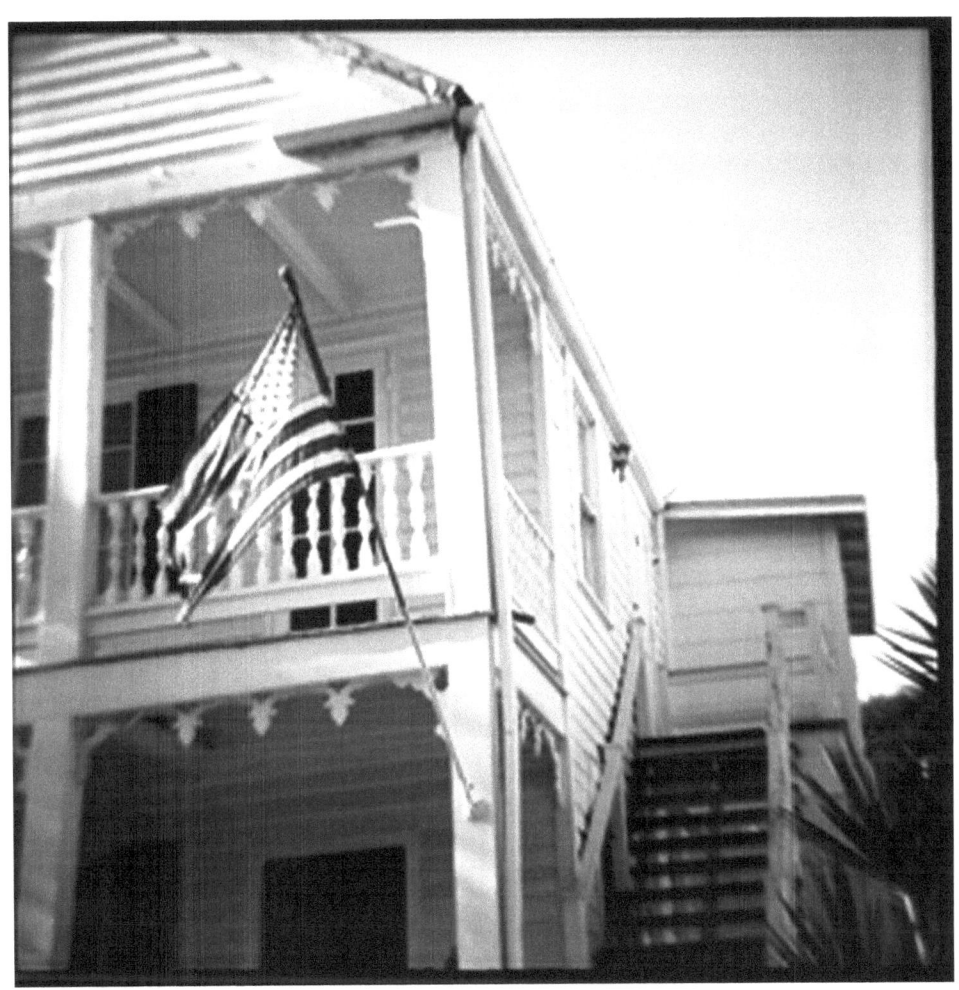

TATTERED FLAG

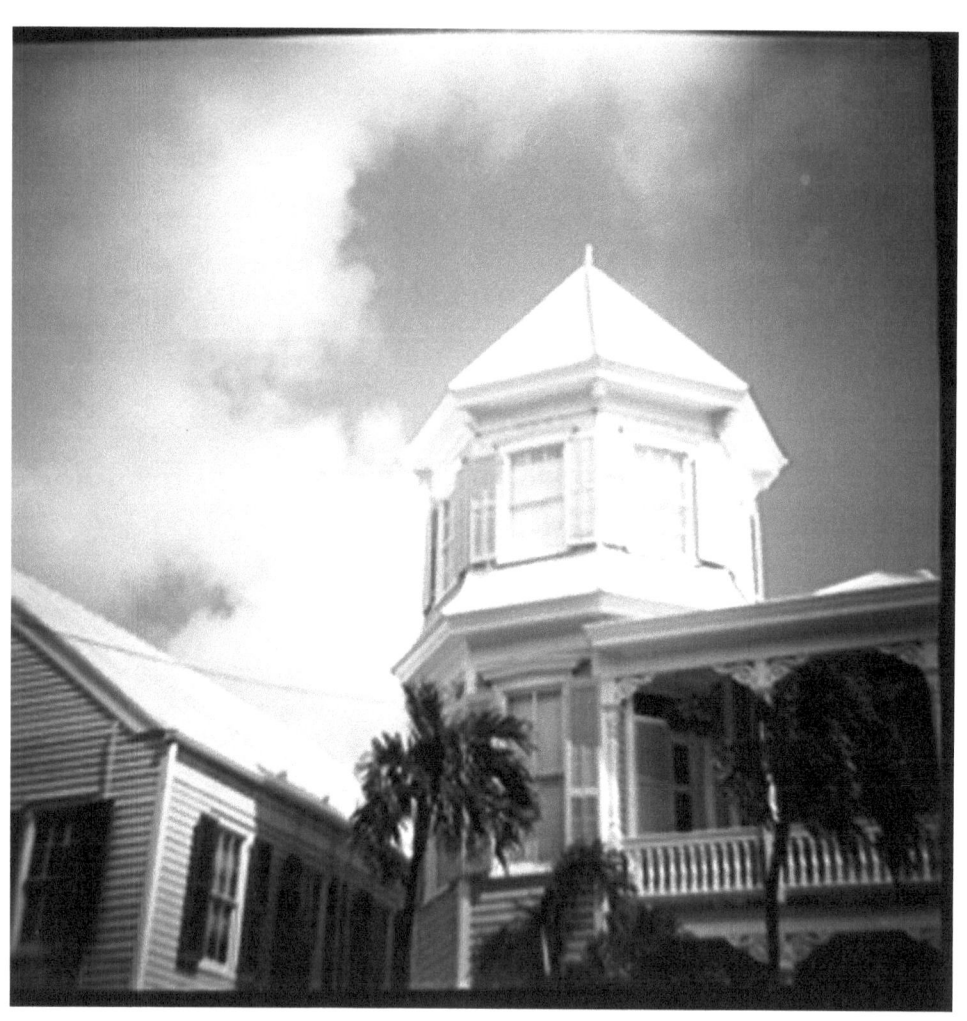

ARTIST HOUSE / OTTO HOUSE

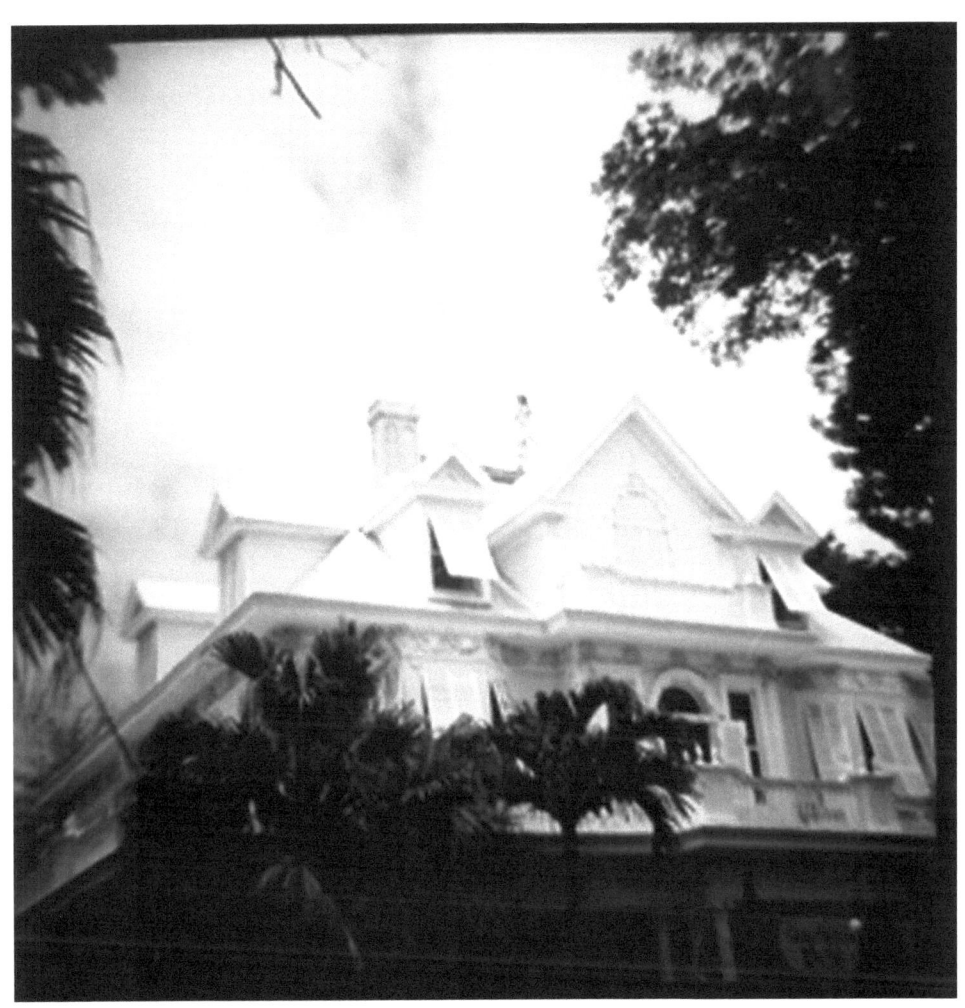

CURRY MANSION

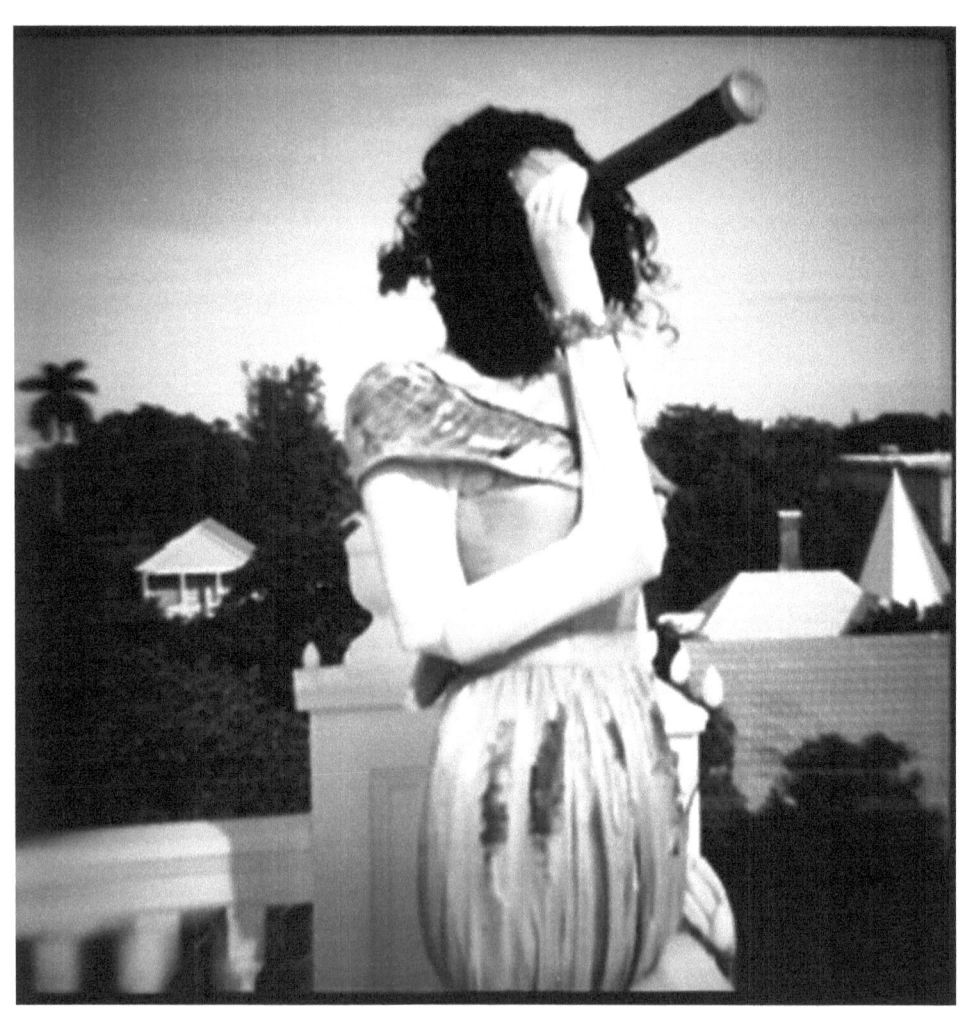

WIDOW'S WALK
Curry Mansion

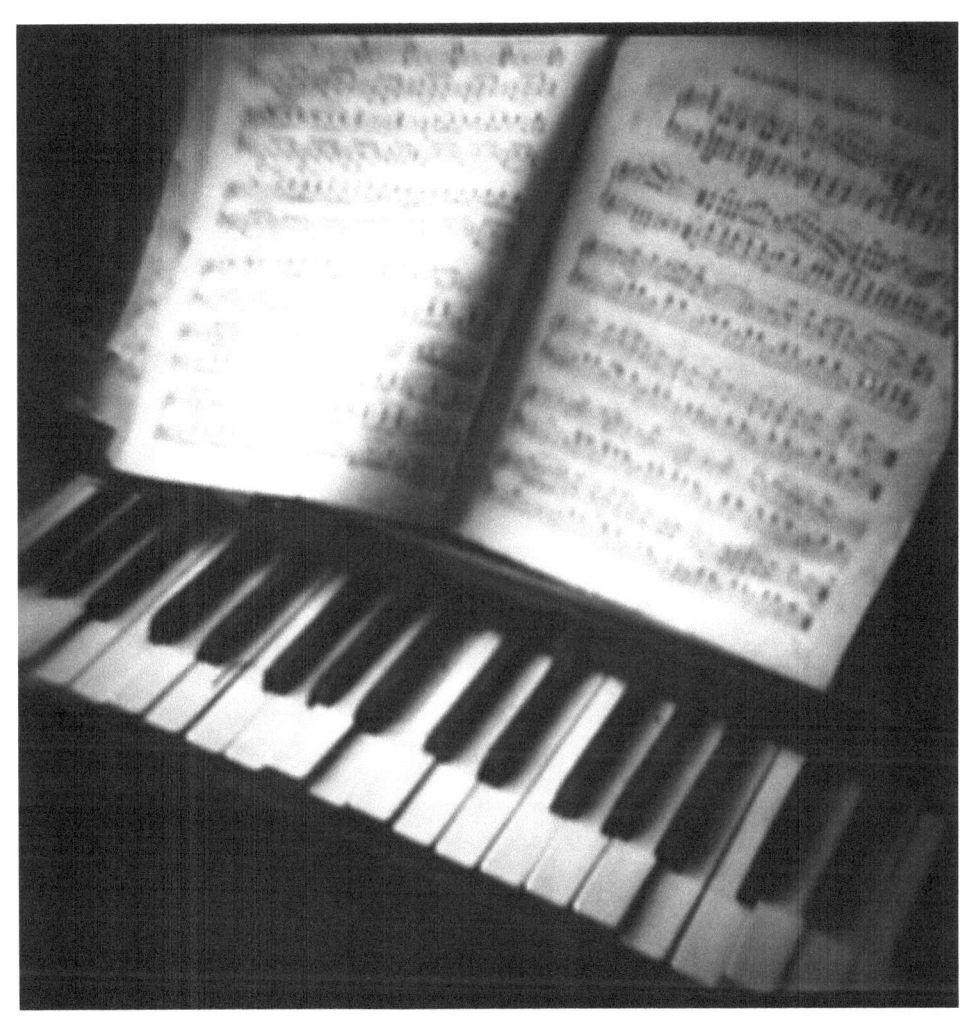

ANTIQUE PIANO
CURRY MANSION

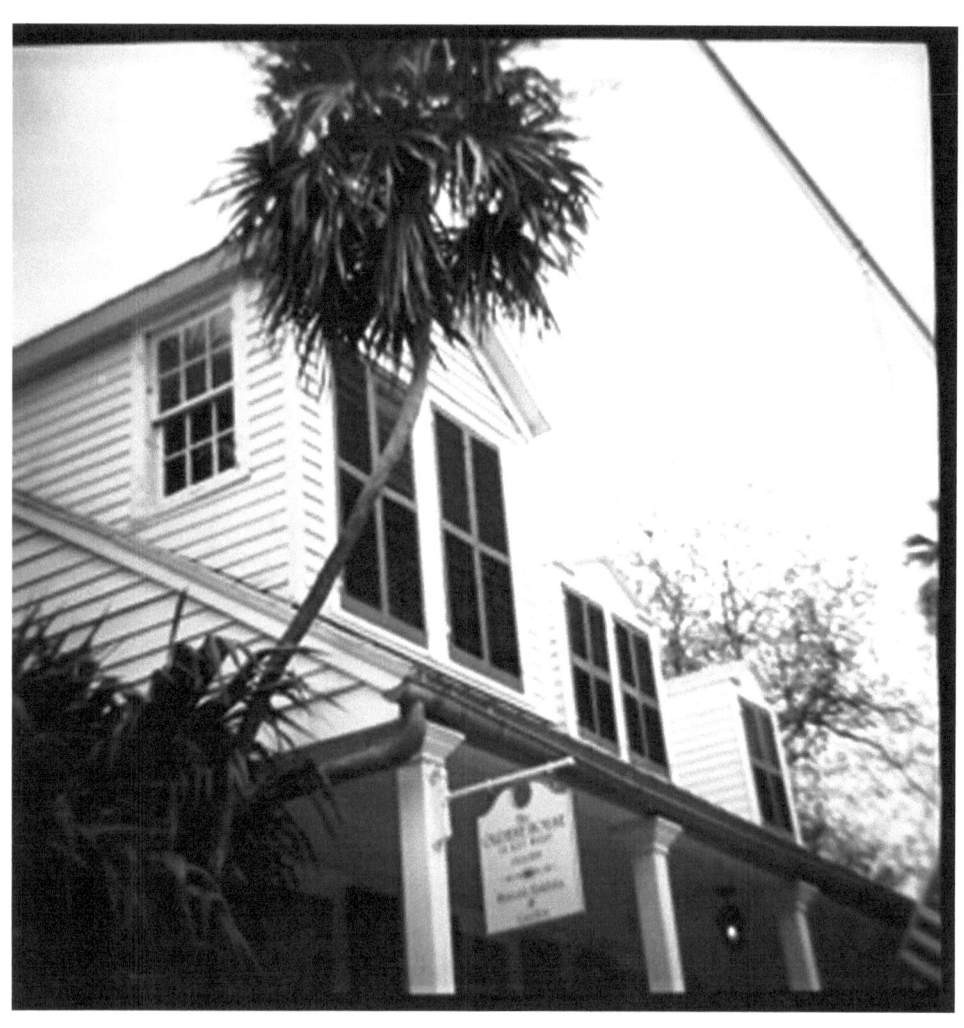

WRECKER'S MUSEUM
Oldest House

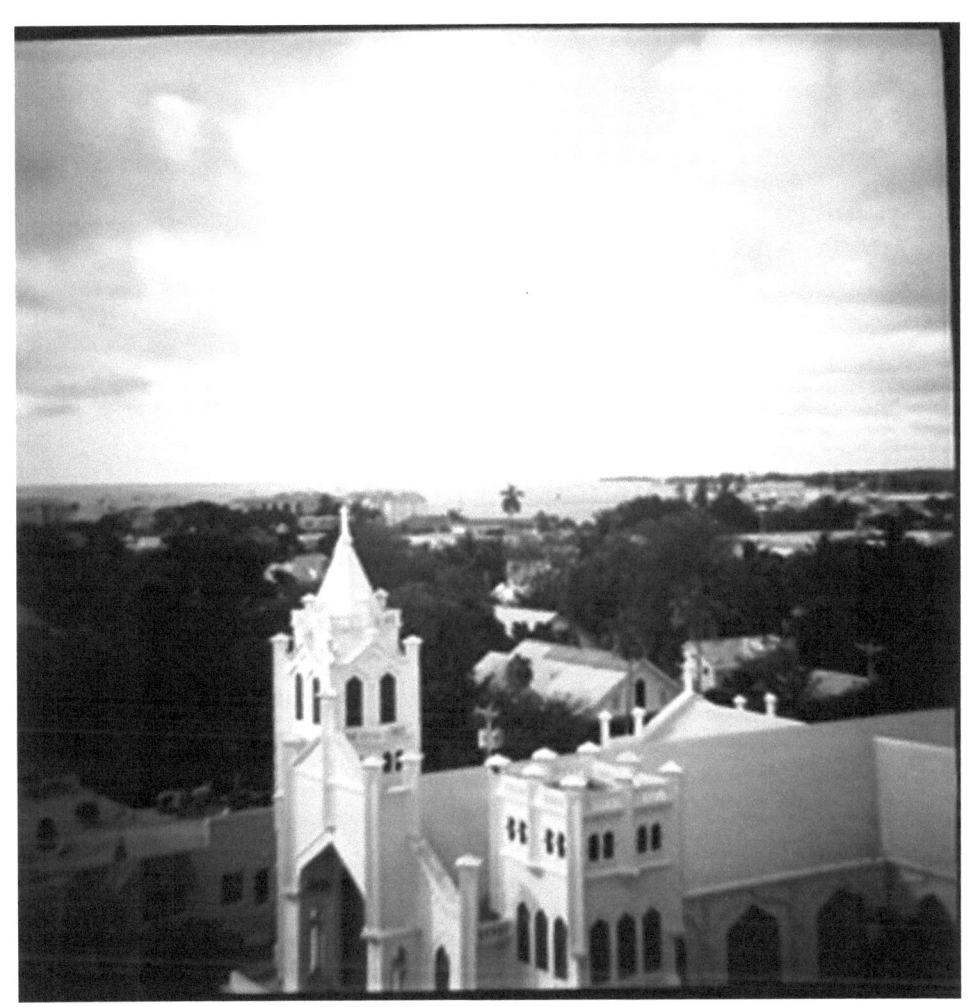

ST. PAUL'S CHURCH

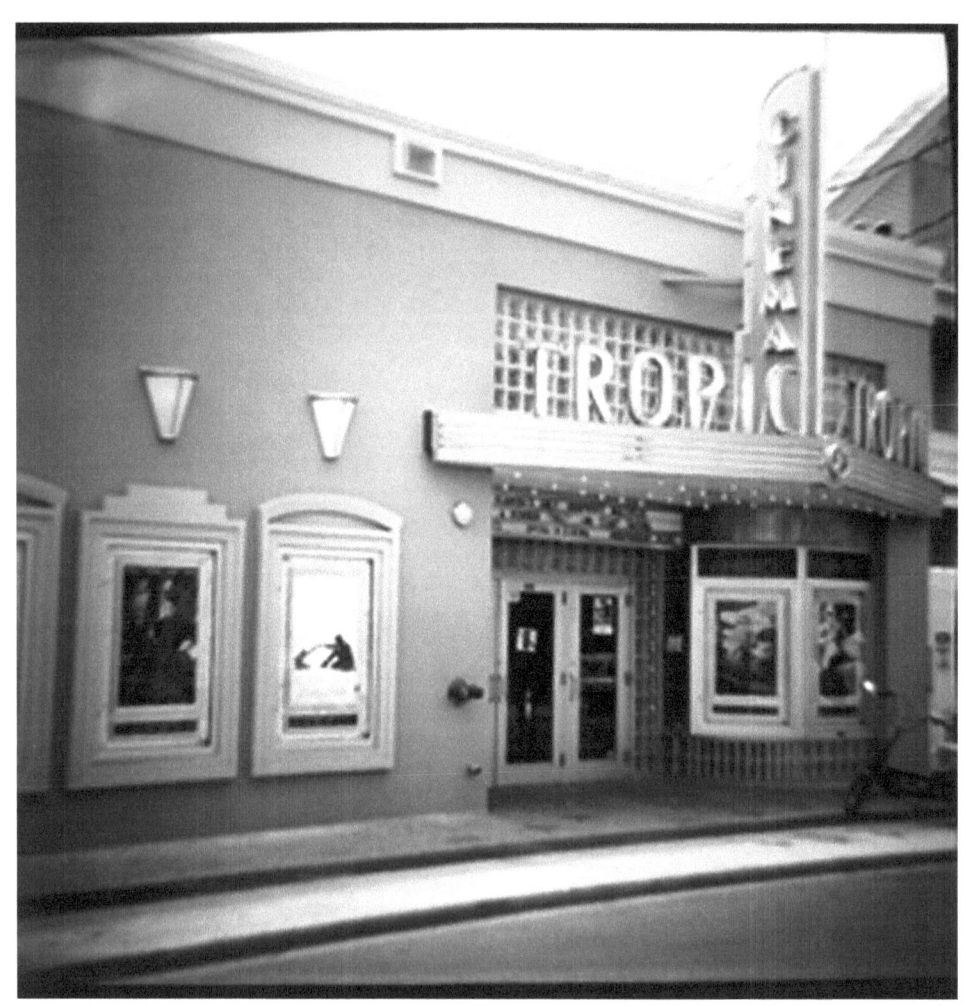

TROPIC CINEMA

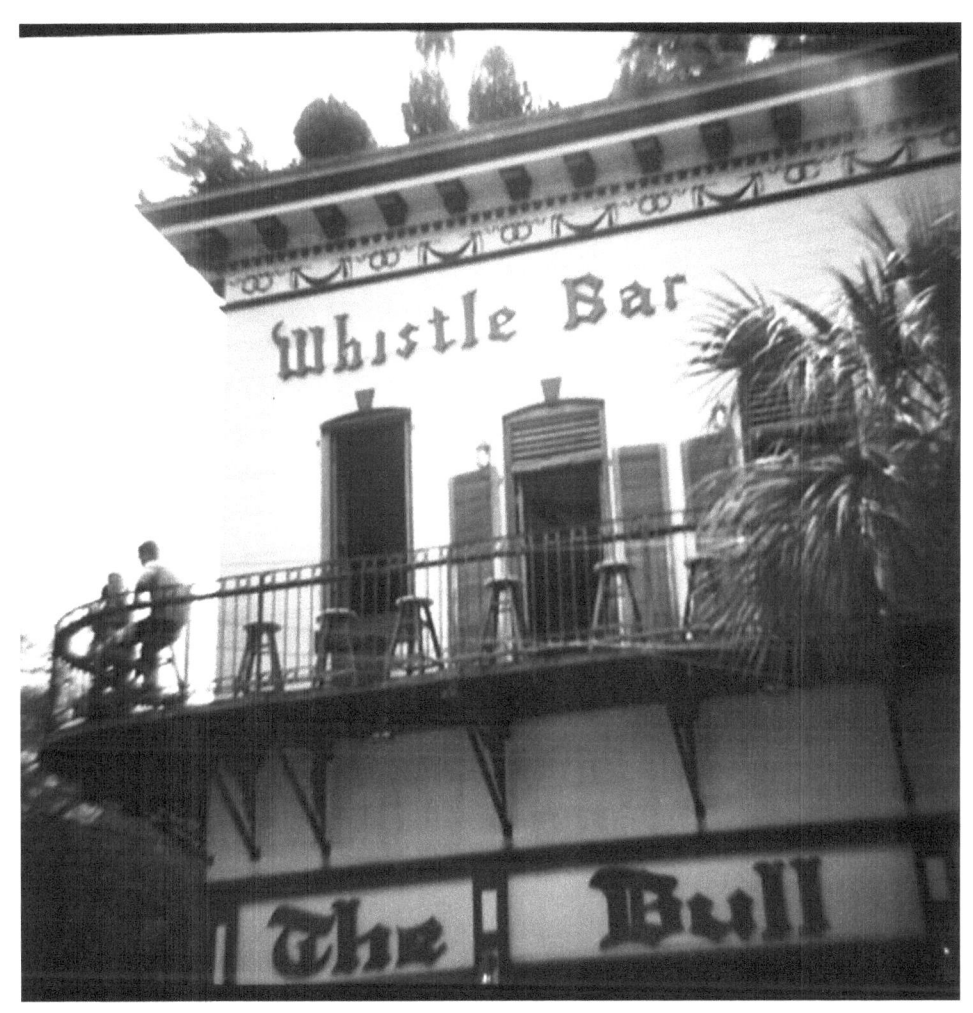

THE BULL AND WHISTLE

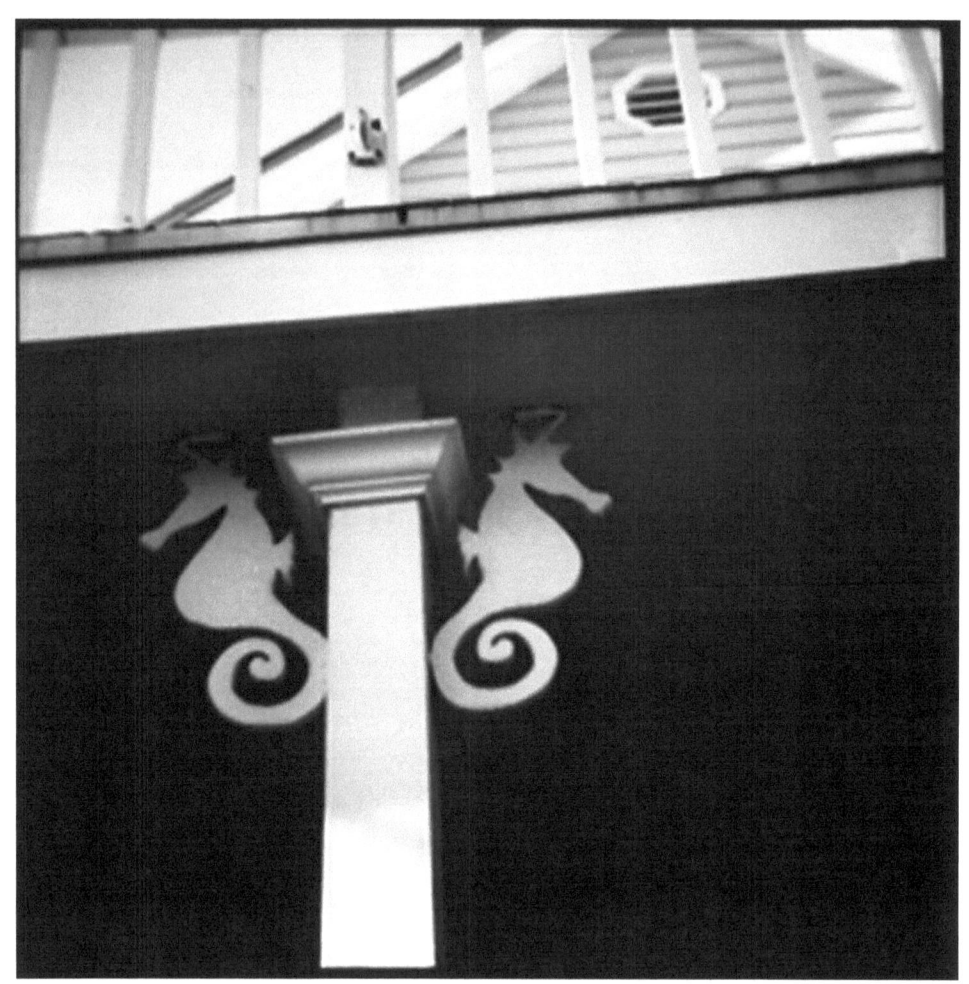

SEA HORSES

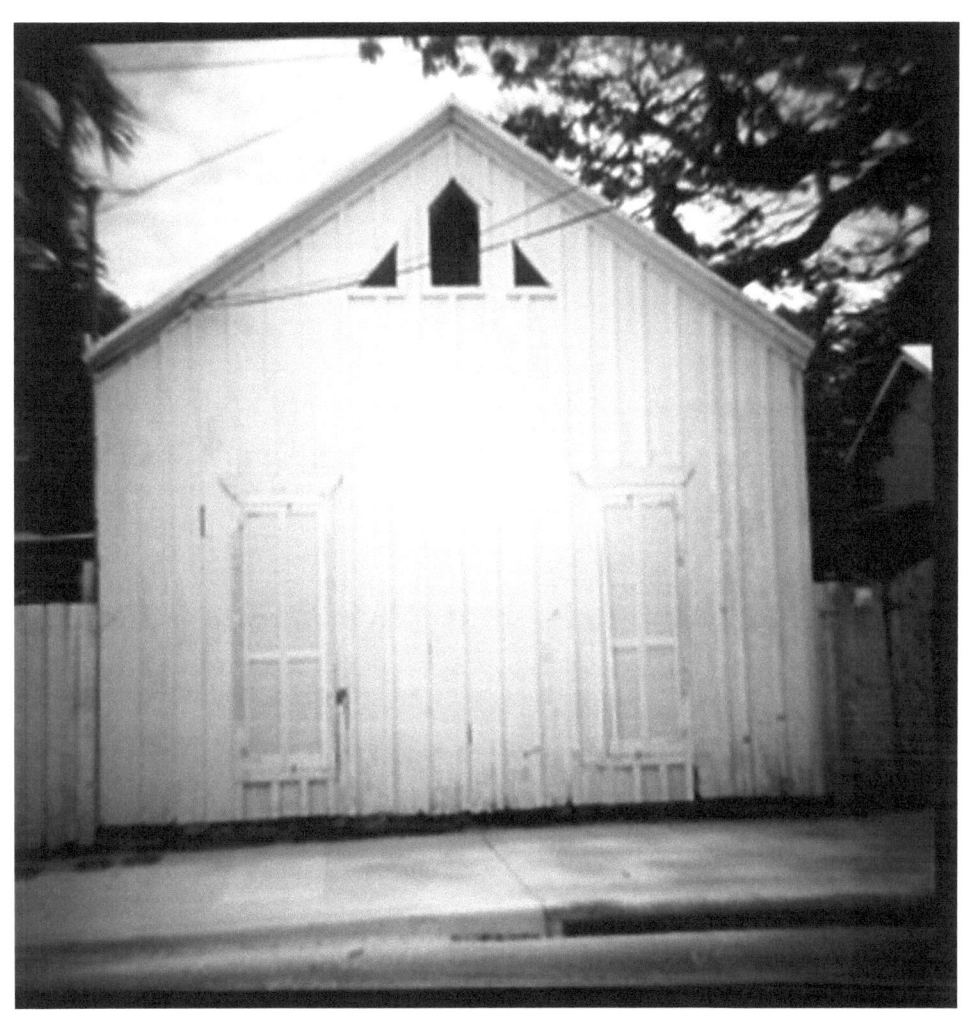

WHITE HOUSE

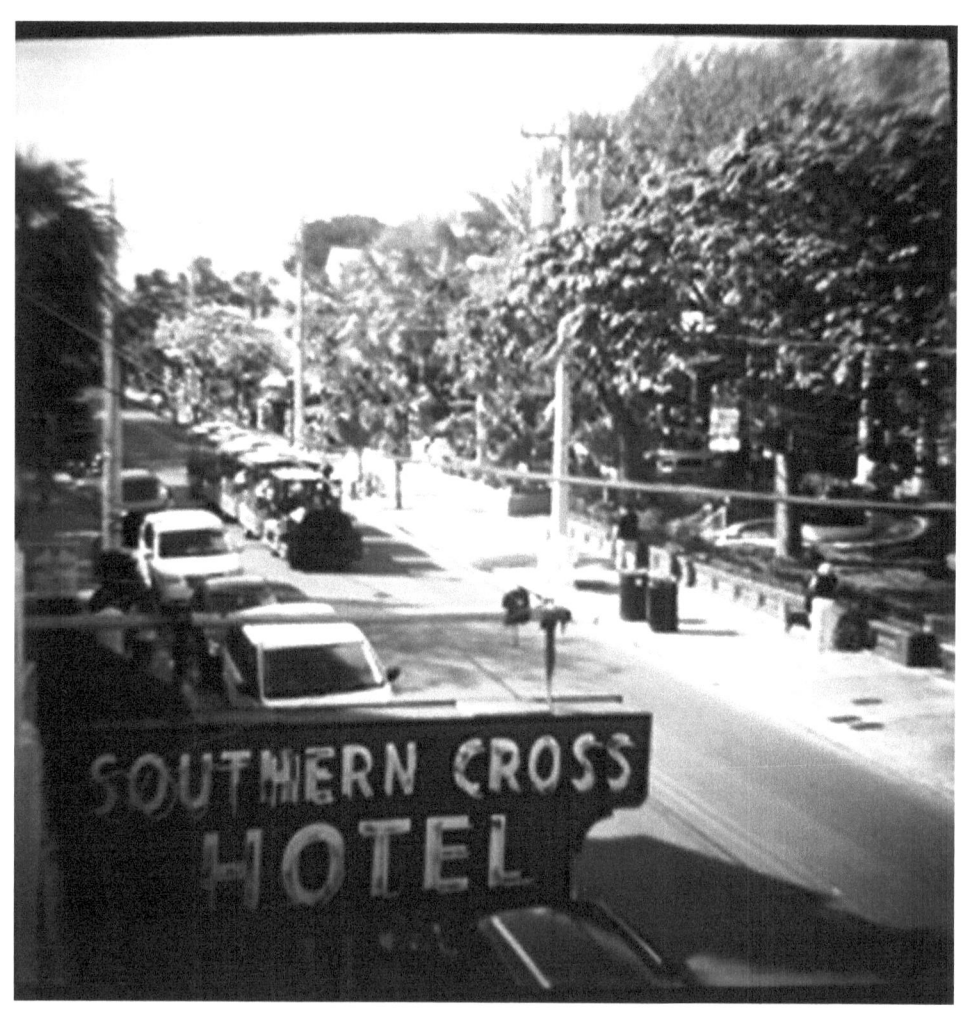

CONCH TRAIN ON DUVAL ST

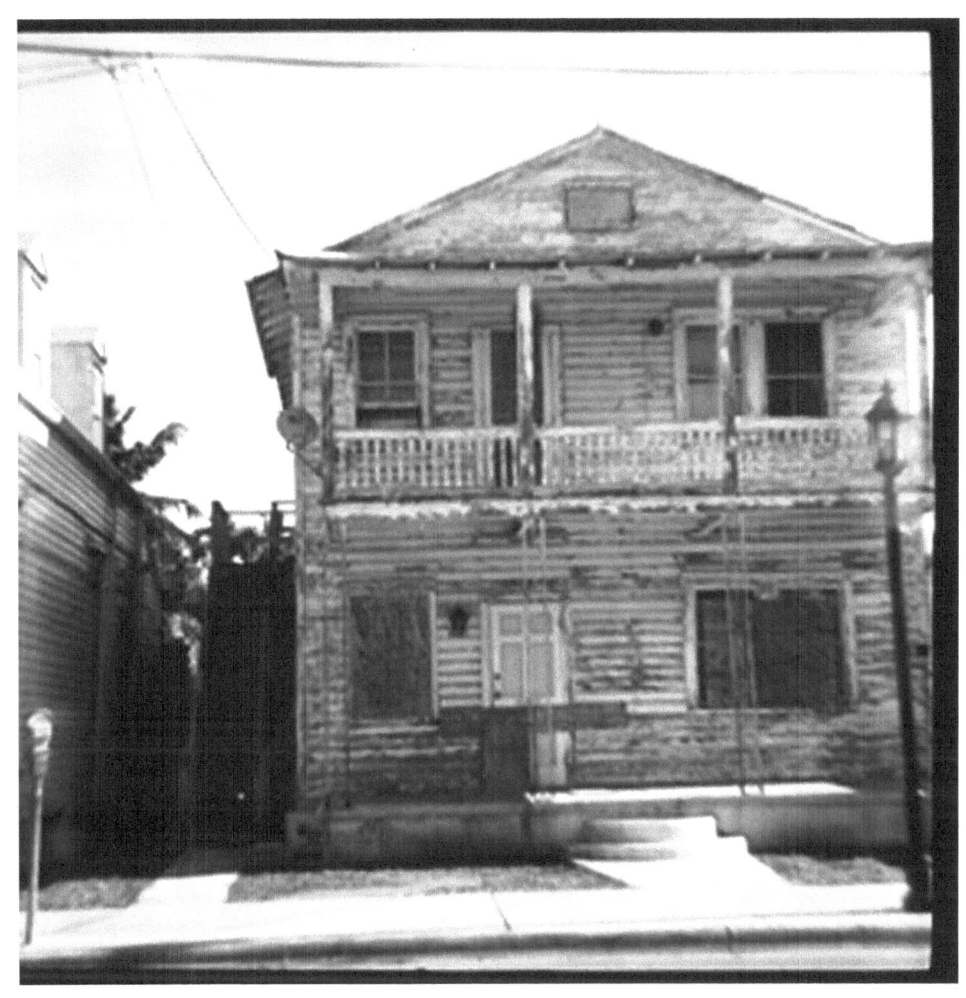

WEATHERED HOUSE

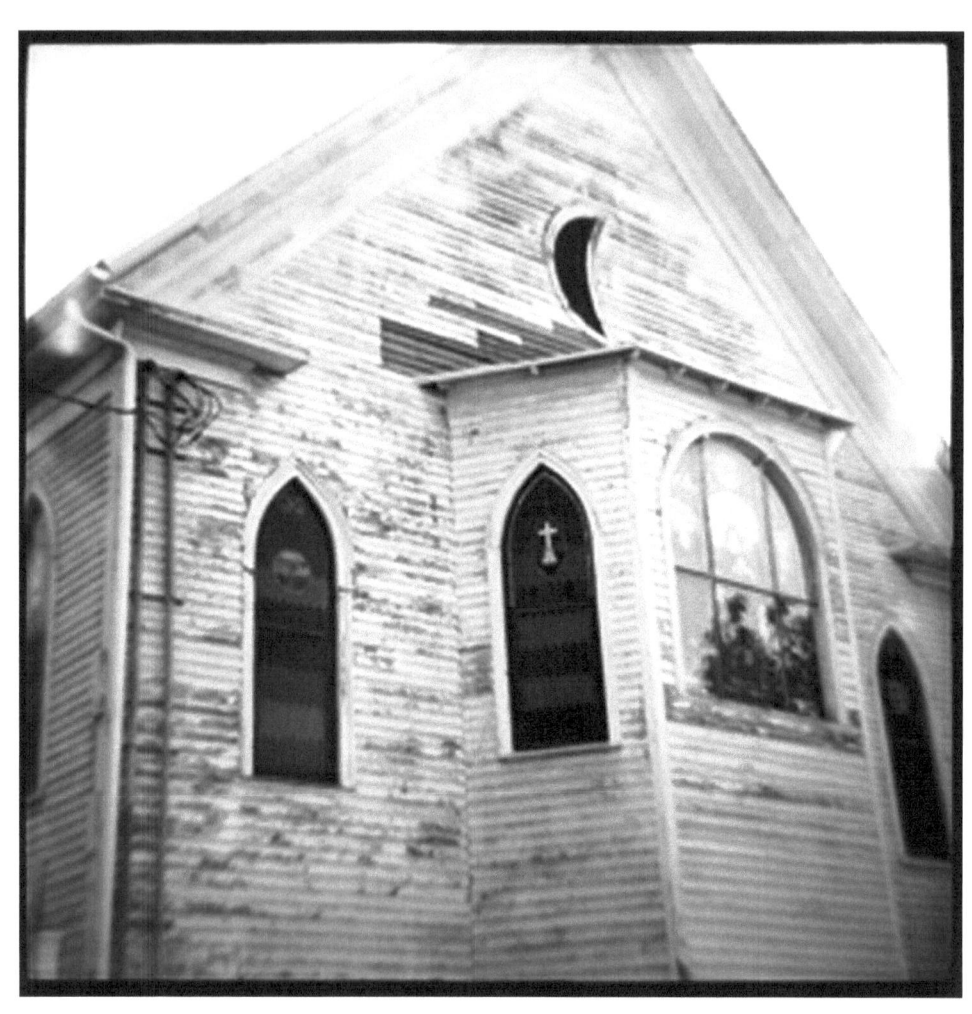

OLD CHURCH BUILDING

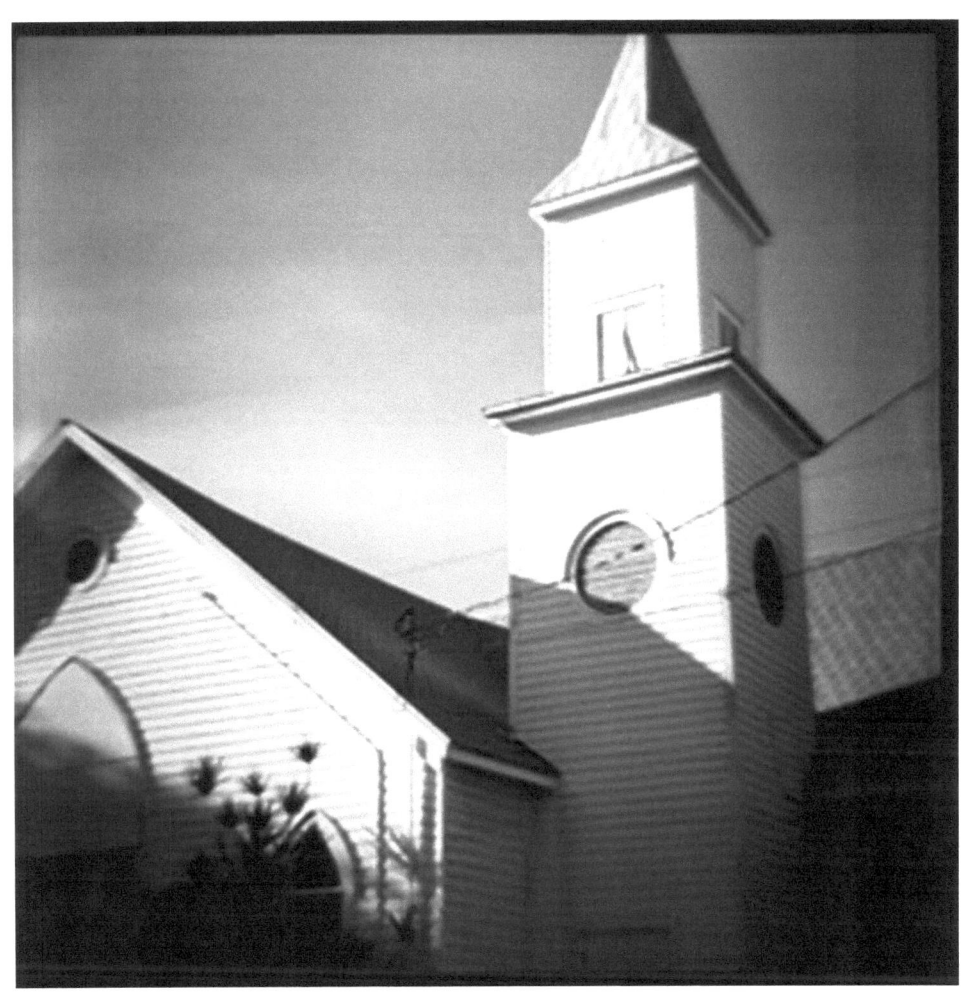

NEWMAN METHODIST CHURCH

TRINITY PRESBYTERIAN CHURCH

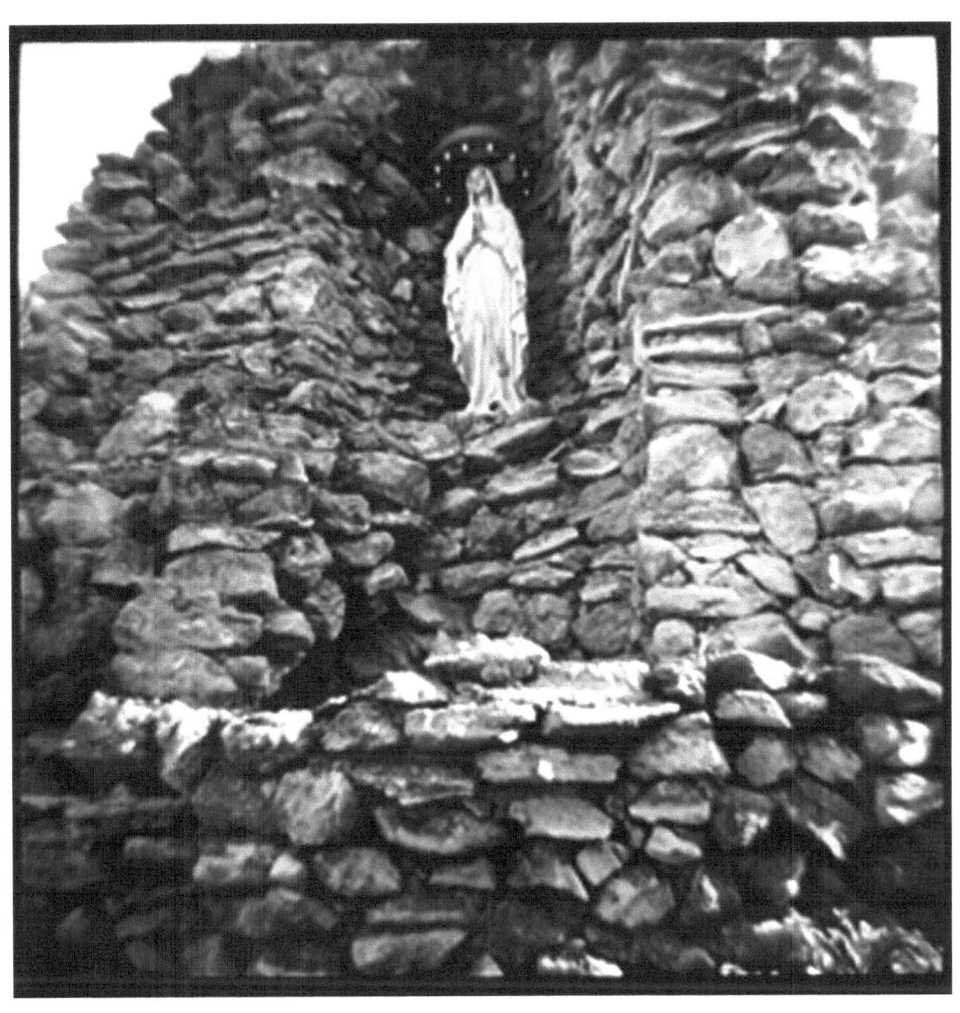

GROTTO SHRINE
St Mary Star of the Sea

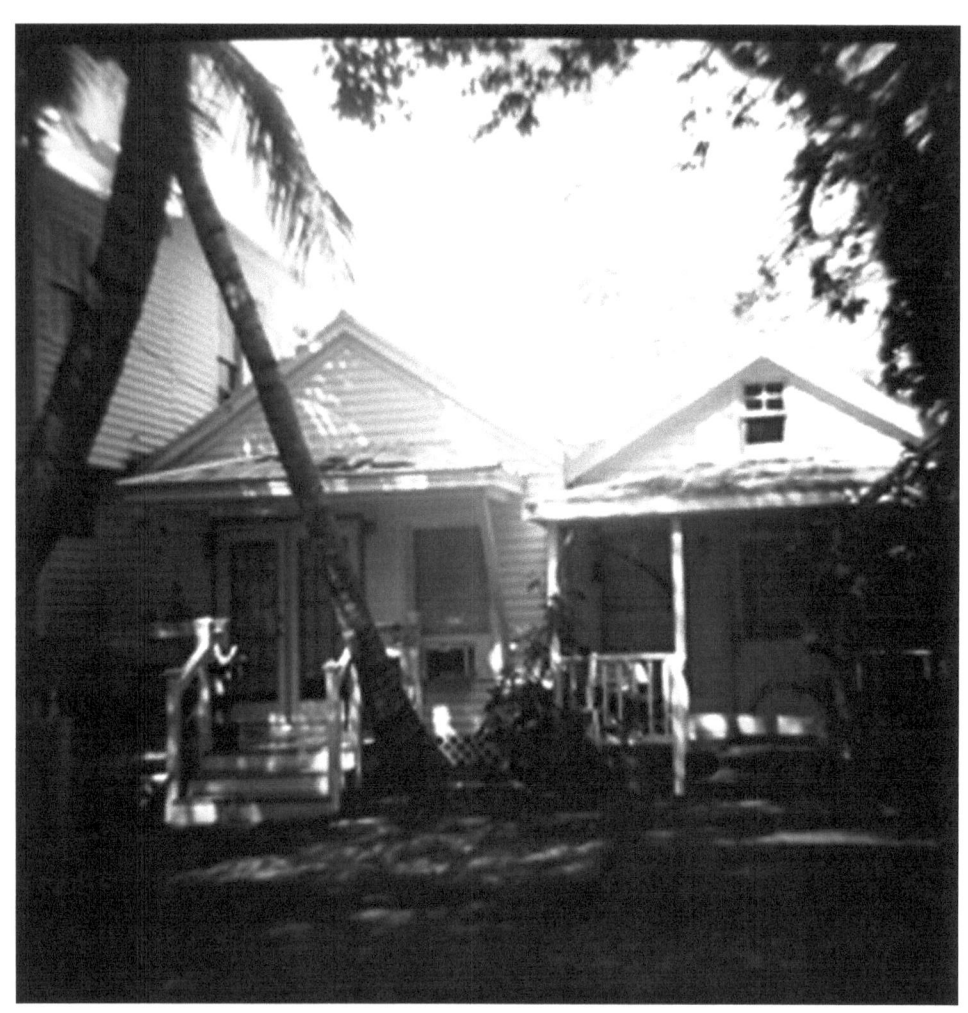

TWO HOUSES

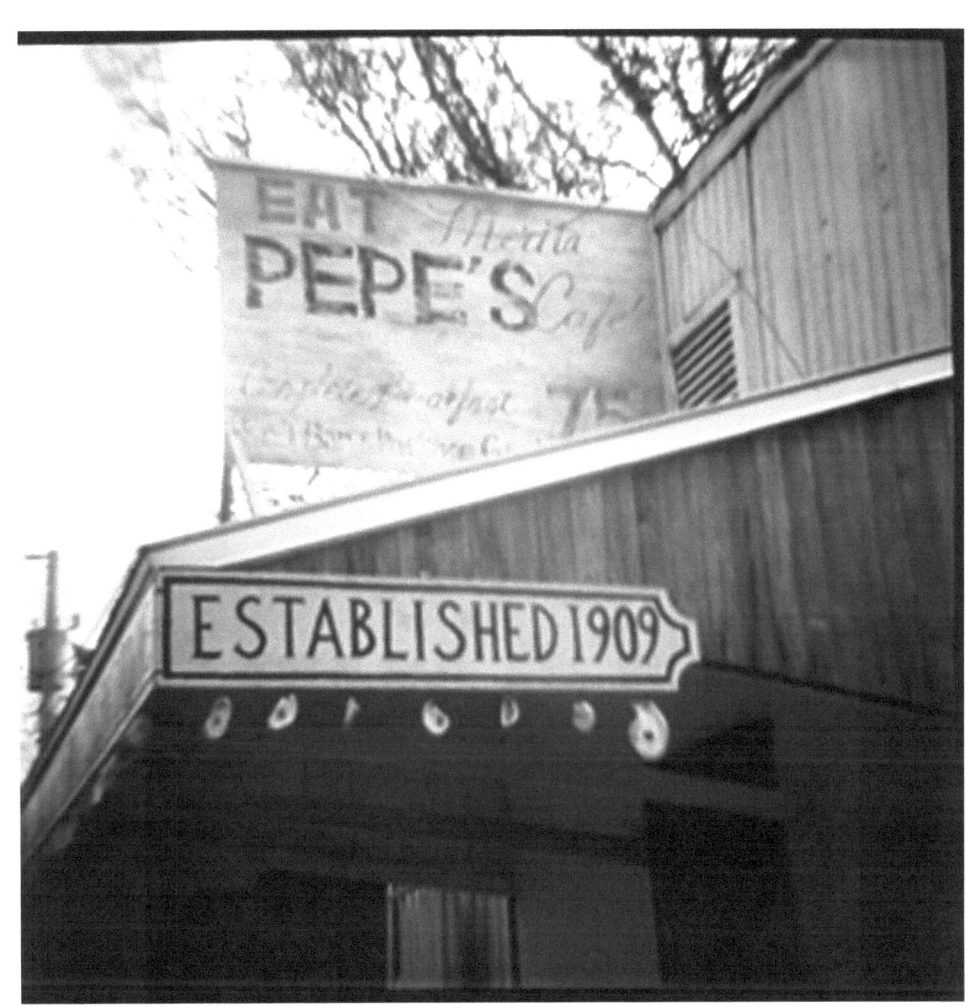

PEPE'S

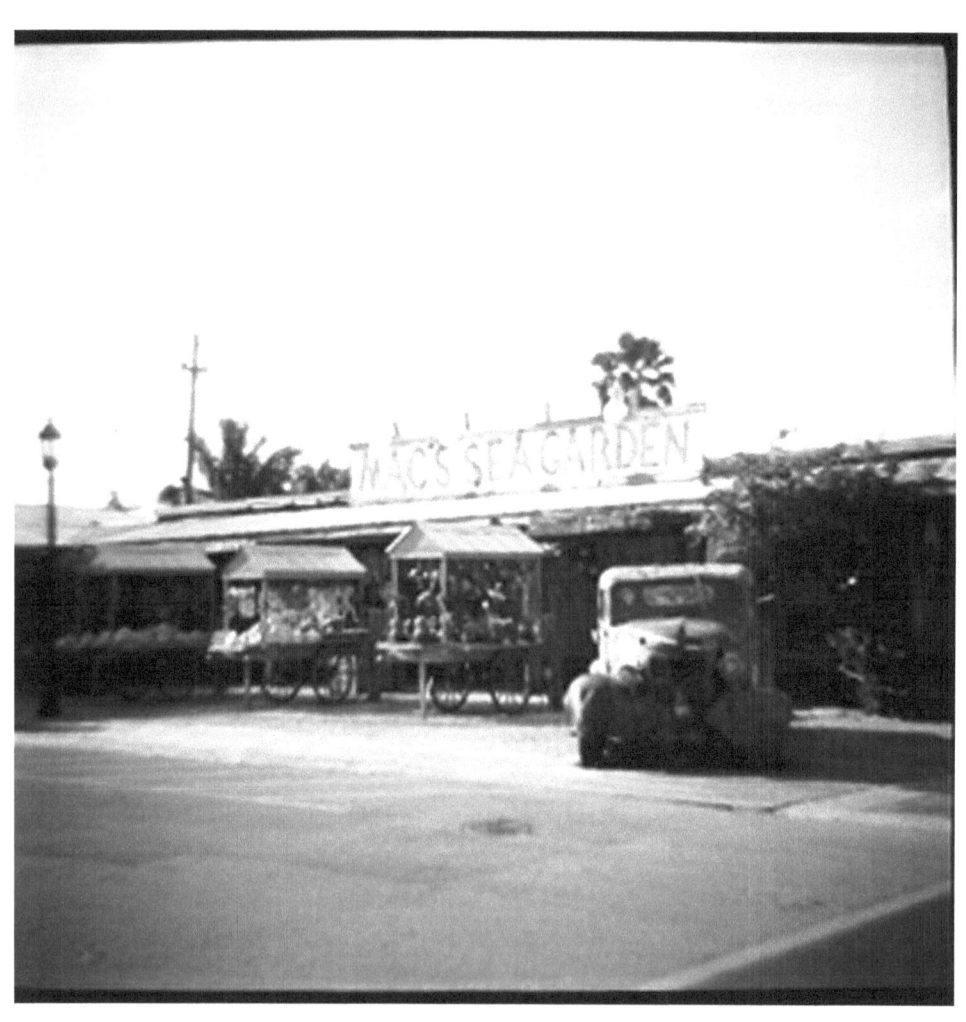

MAC'S SEA GARDEN

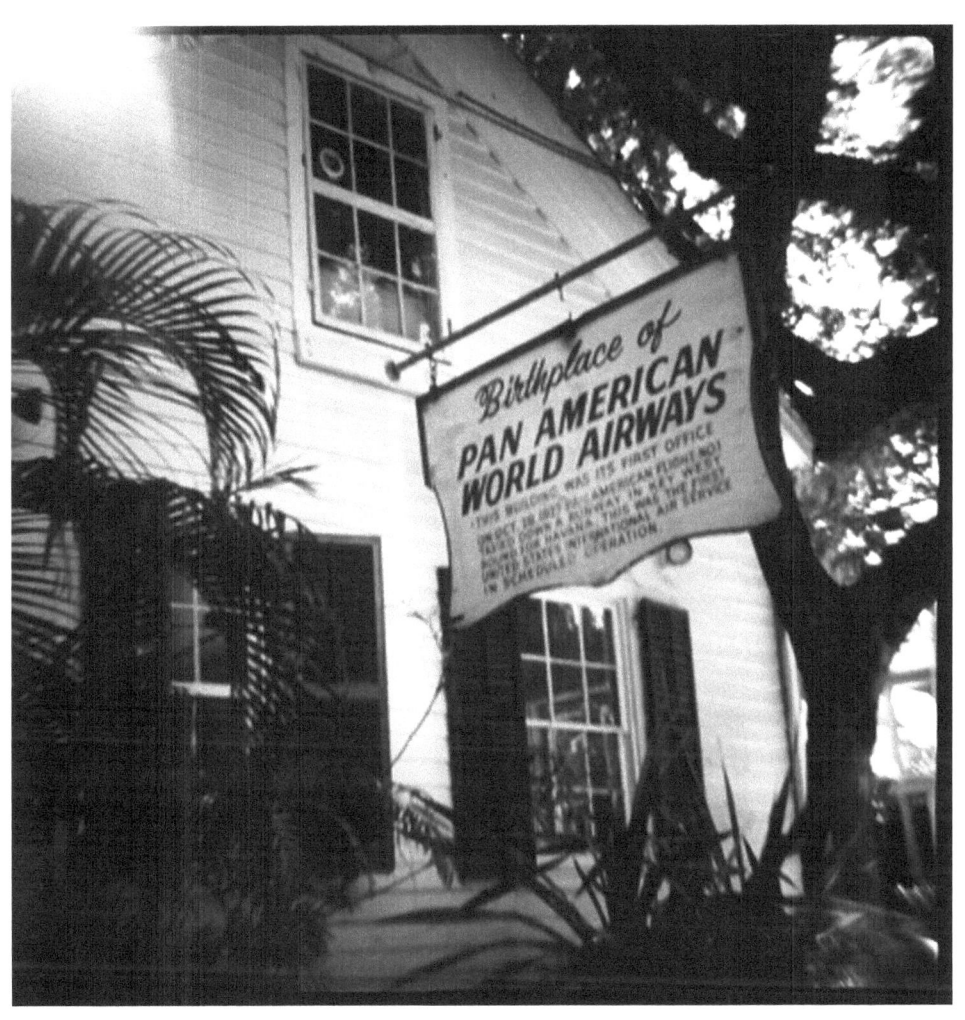

BIRTHPLACE OF PAN AM
NOW HOME TO KELLY'S CARRIBEAN BAR

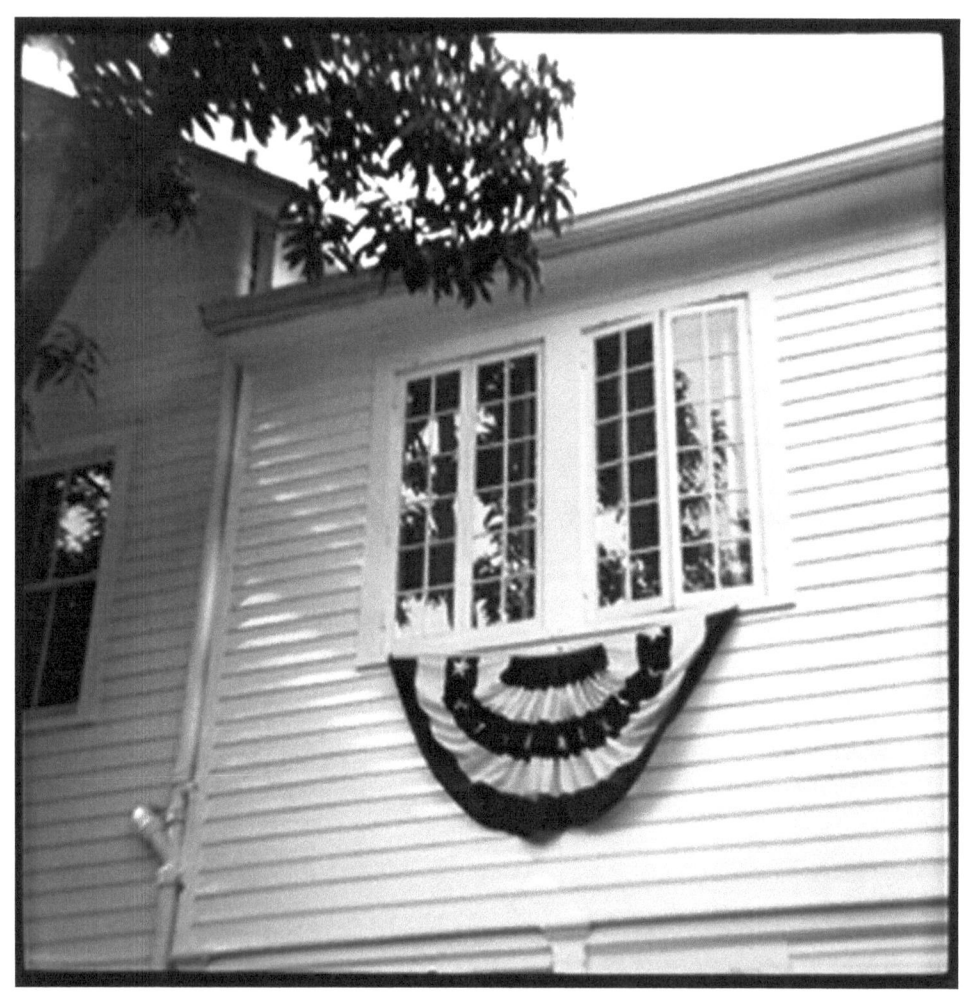

HARRY S. TRUMAN LITTLE WHITE HOUSE

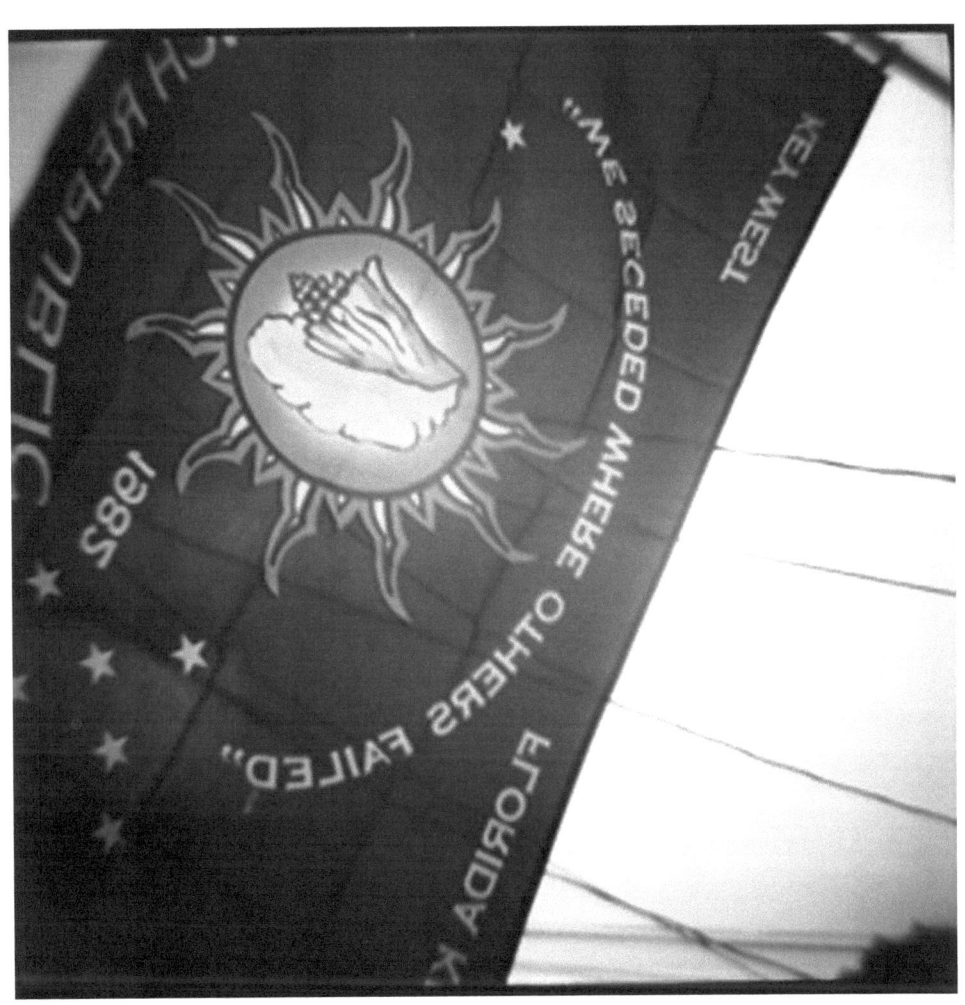

CONCH REPUBLIC FLAG

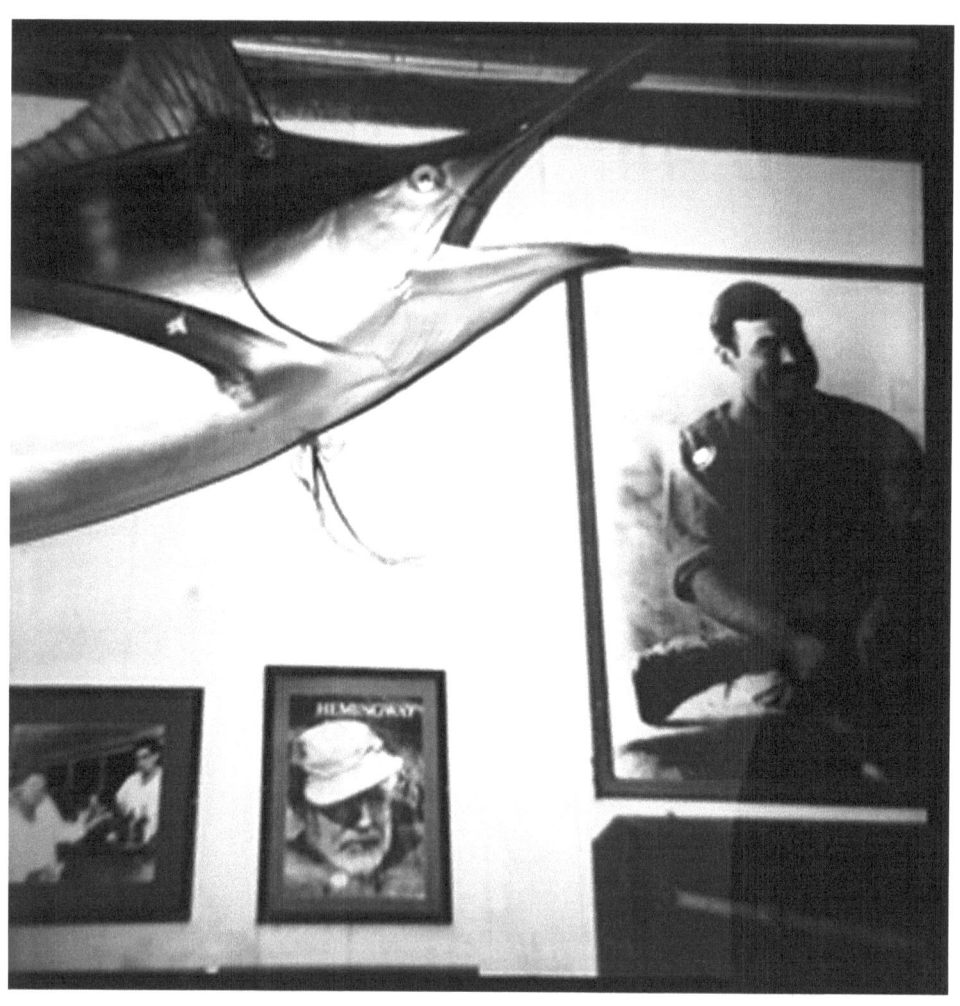

HEMINGWAY MEMORABILIA
SLOPPY JOE'S BAR

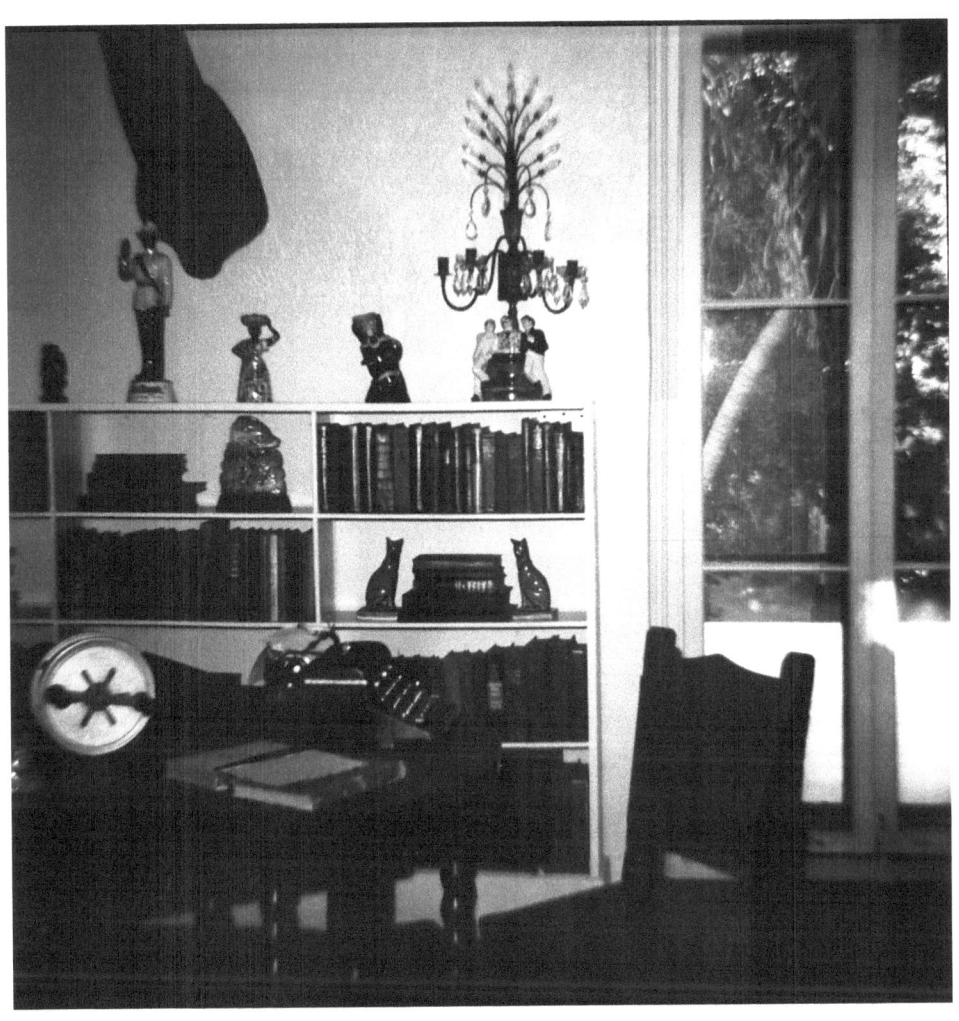

HEMINGWAY STUDY
Hemingway Home

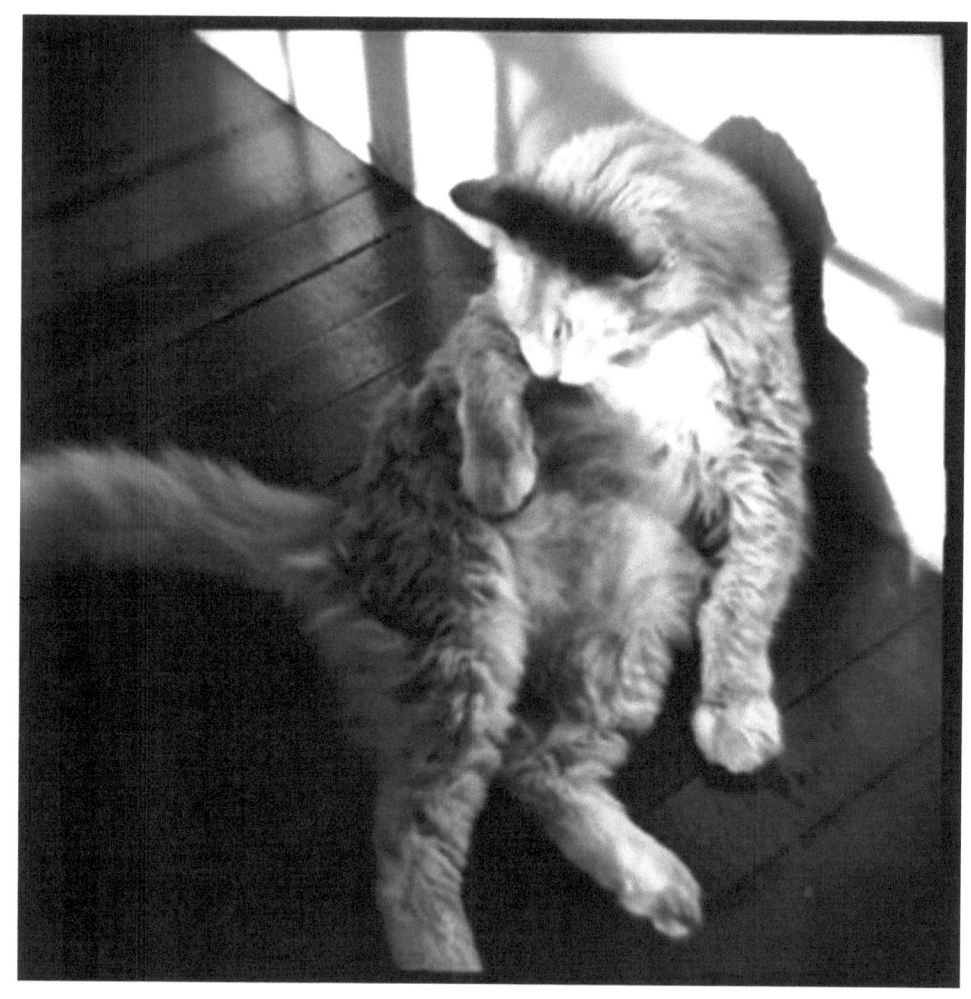

ARCHIE
HEMINGWAY HOME

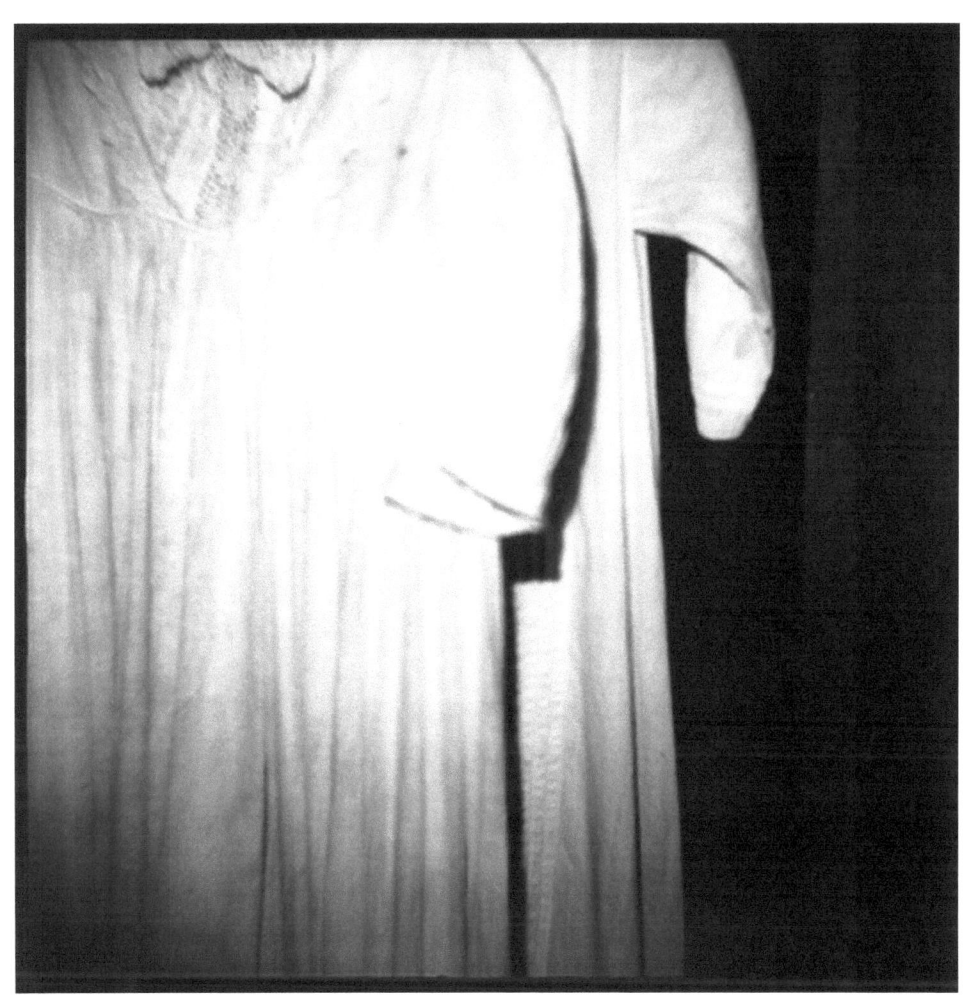

NIGHTGOWNS
Audubon House

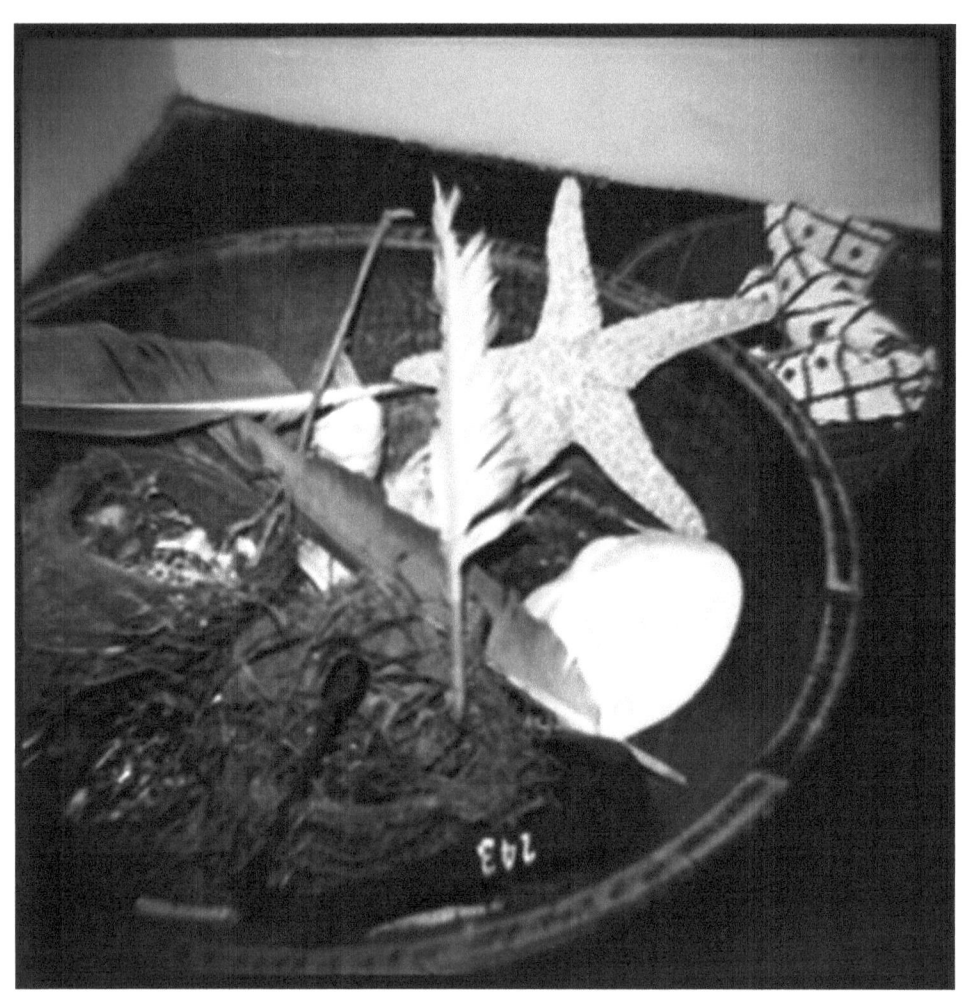

STARFISH AND FEATHERS
Audubon House

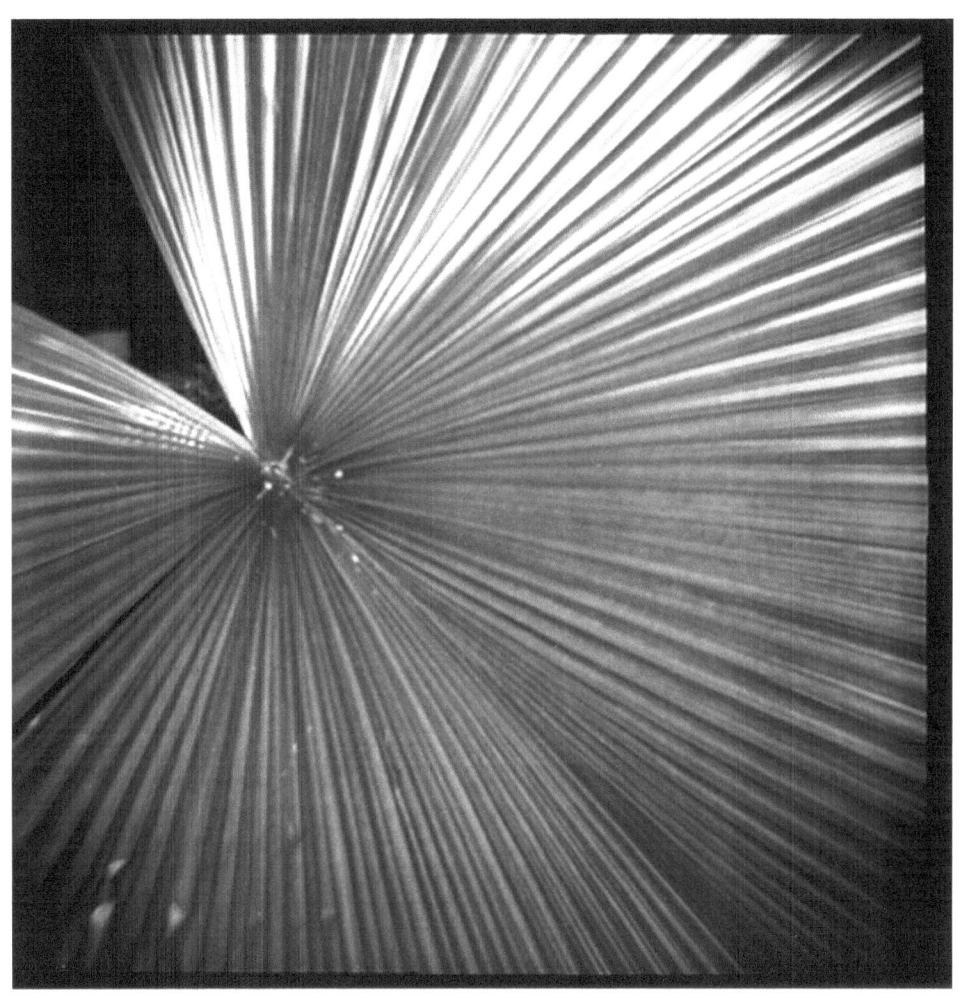

PALM FROND

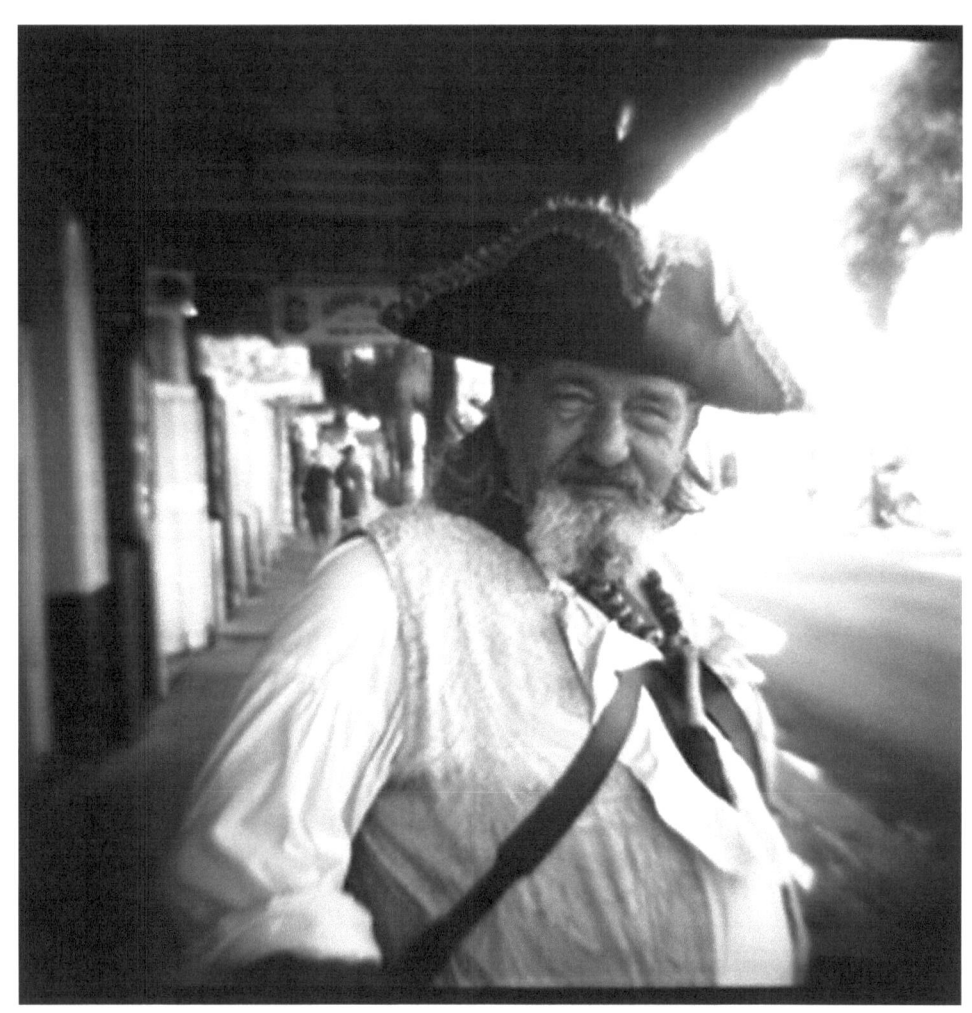

CAPT STITCH

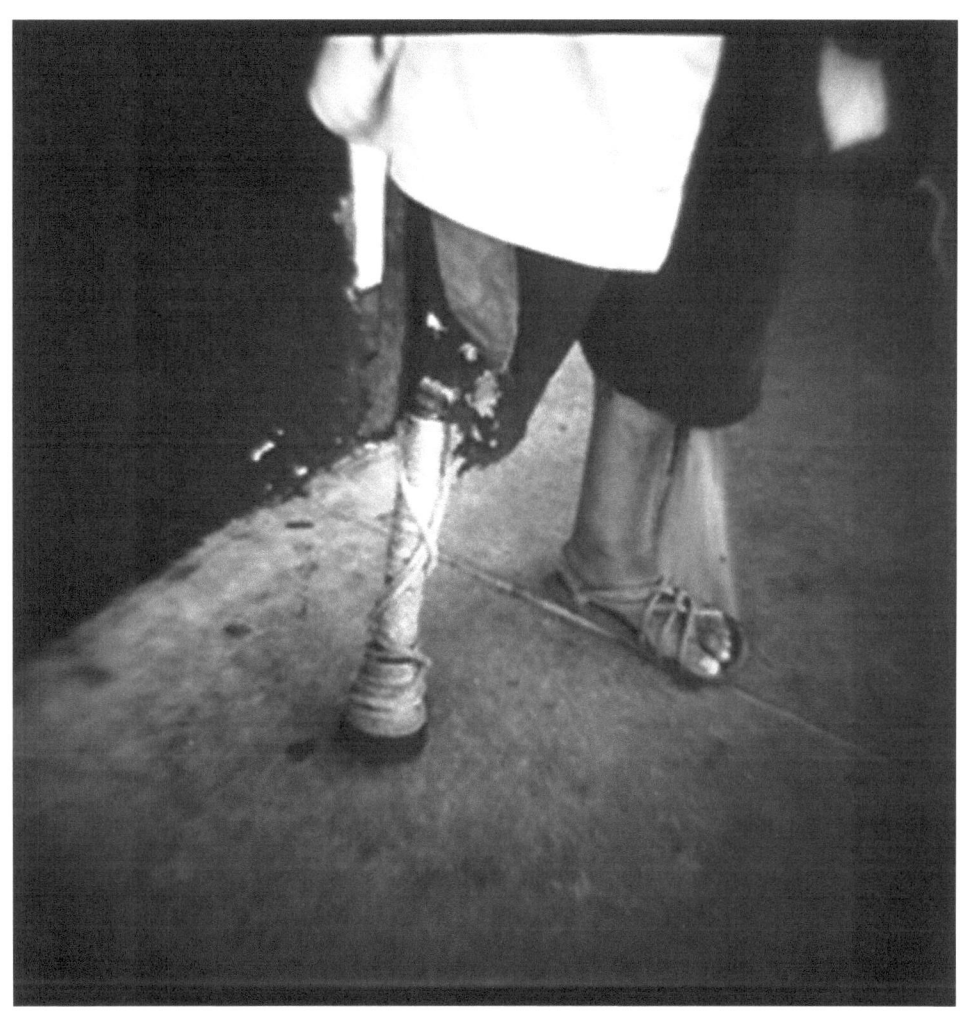

PEG LEG OF CAPT STITCH

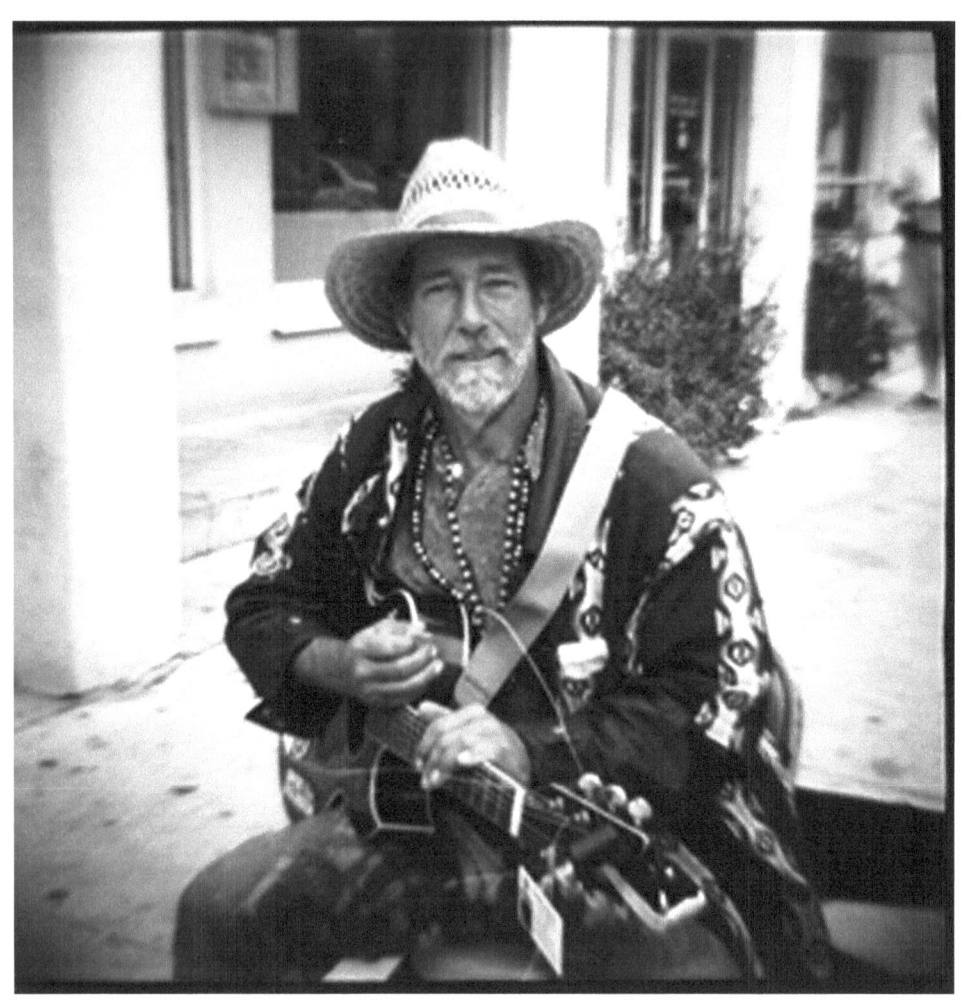

COWBOY GEORGE
STREET MUSICIAN

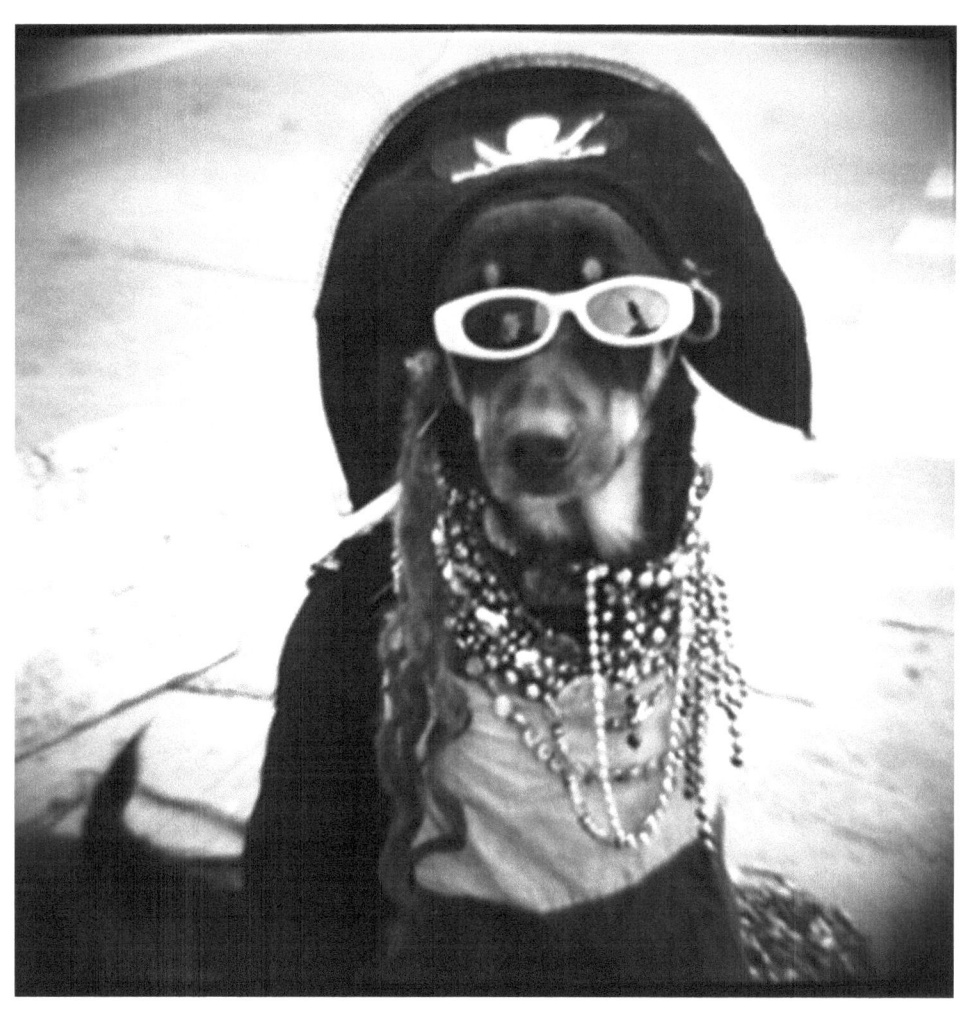

MONSTER THE MAGNIFICENT
Sidekick of Cowboy George

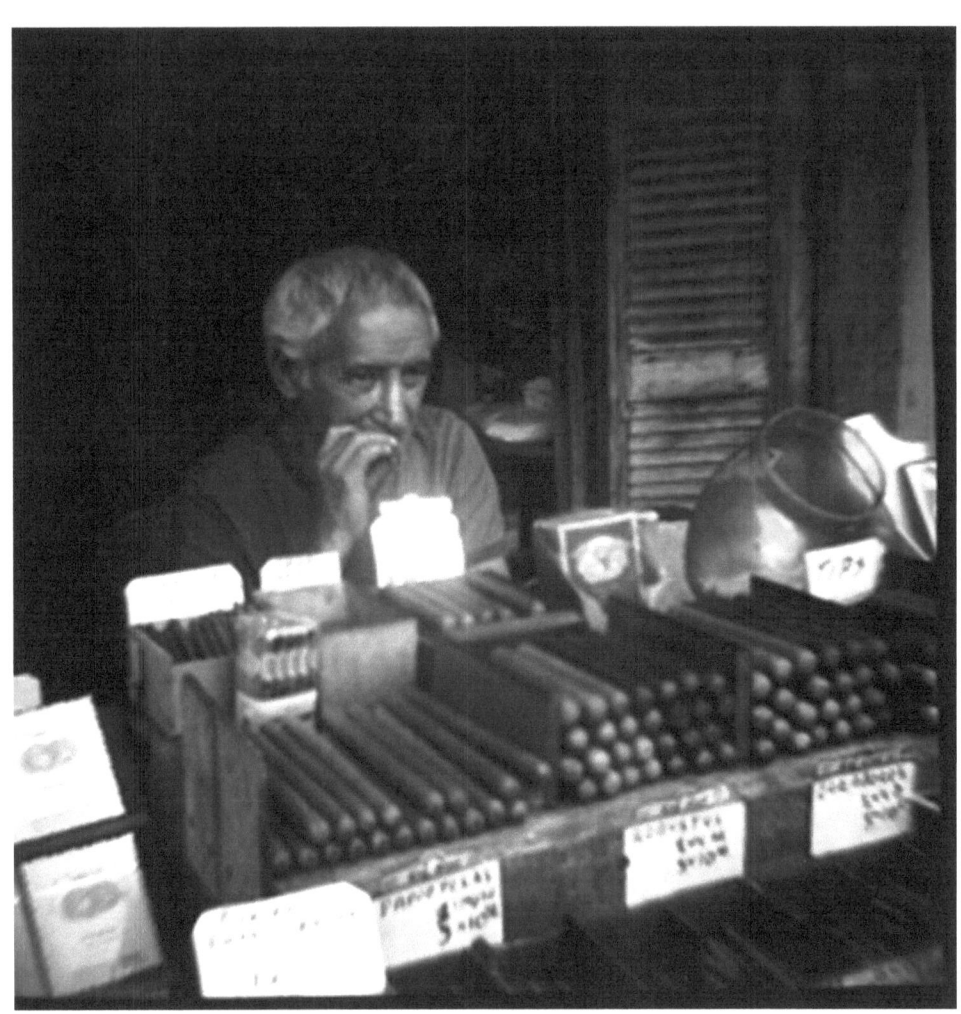

CIGAR SELLER

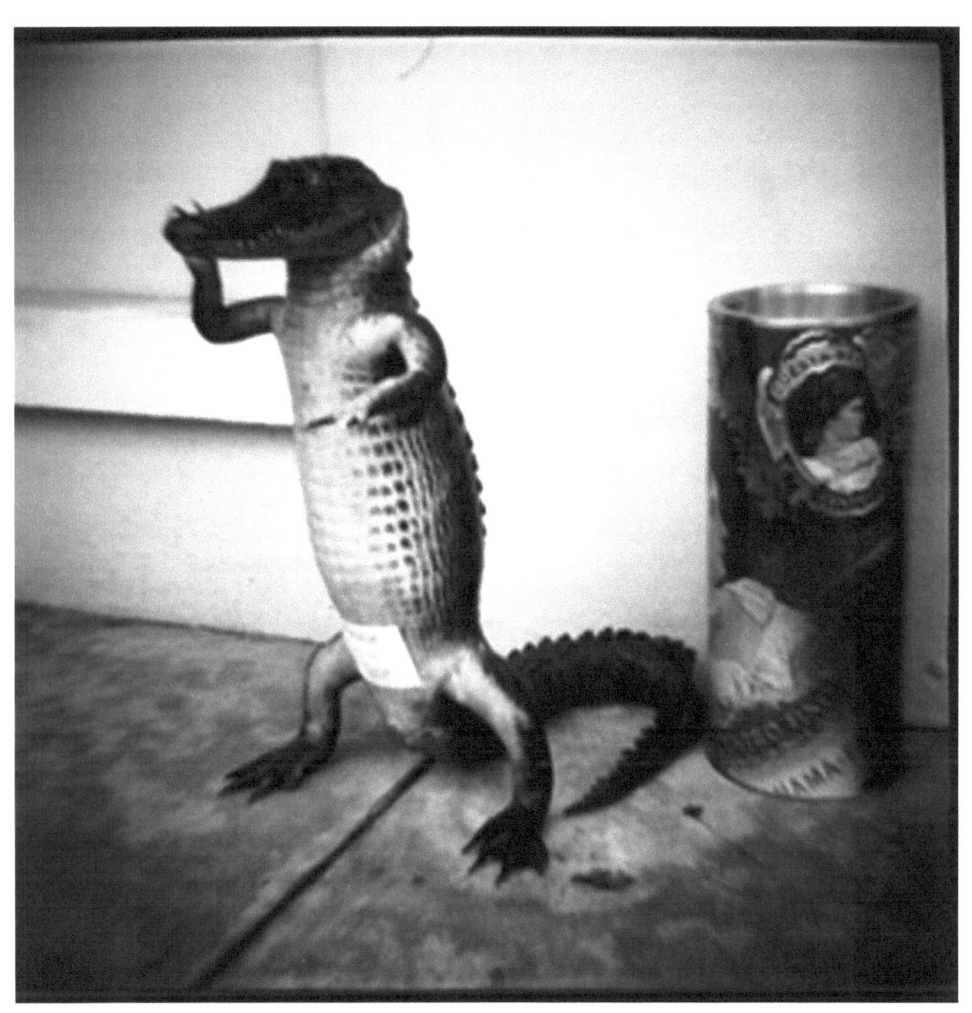

CIGAR STORE ALLIGATOR

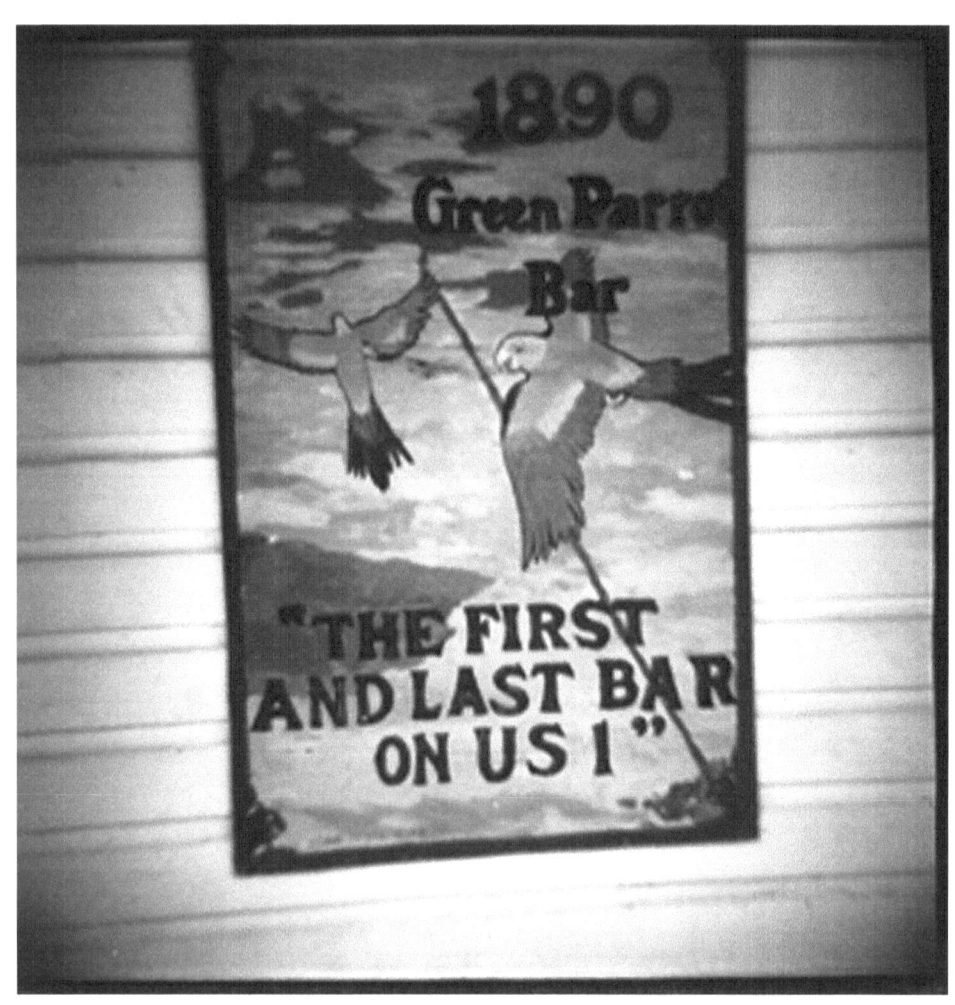

GREEN PARROT BAR

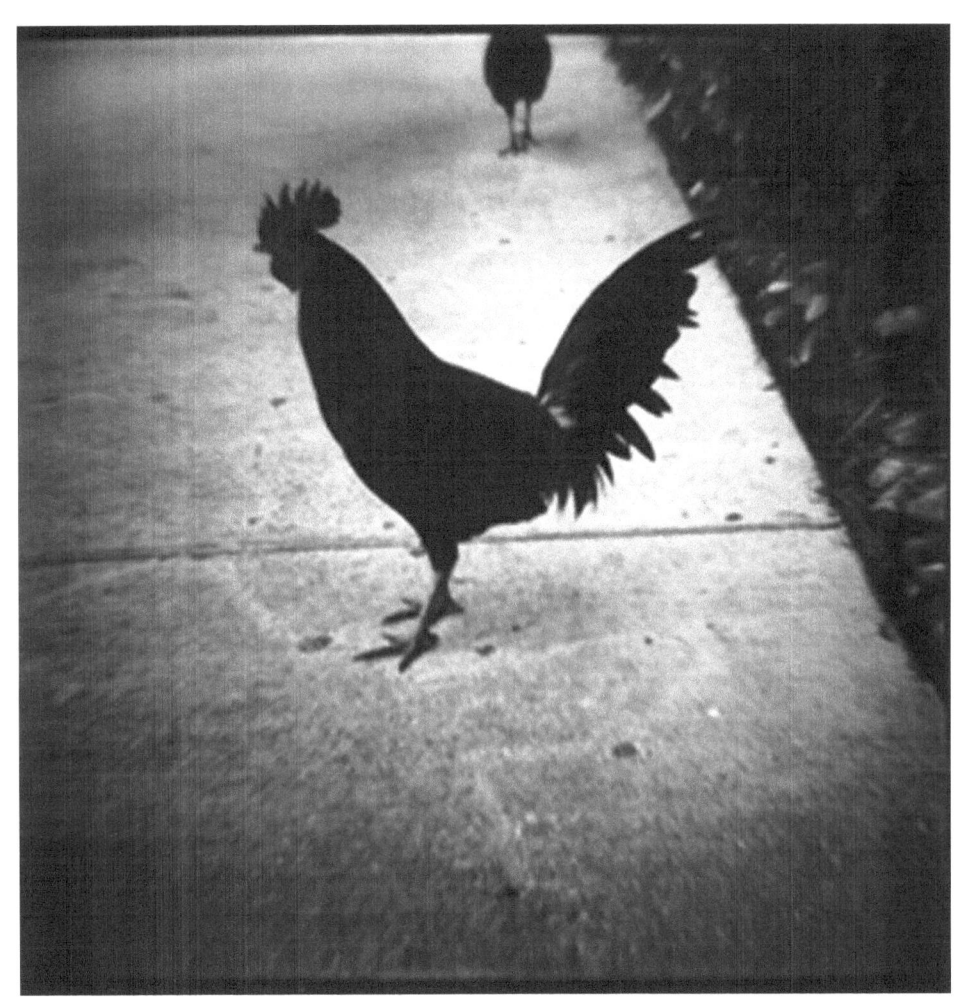

GYPSY ROOSTER

MALLORY SQUARE

MALLORY SQUARE, LOCATED AT THE NORTH END OF DUVAL STREET, IS THE HOME OF THE FAMOUS SUNSET CELEBRATION. THIS TRADITION ORIGINATED IN THE SIXTIES WHEN PEOPLE BEGAN GATHERING TO WATCH THE SUN GO DOWN. IT EVOLVED INTO A CARNIVAL-LIKE EXPERIENCE, WITH STREET PERFORMERS AND LOCAL CRAFTSMEN PROVIDING ENTERTAINMENT UNTIL THE SPECTACULAR SUNSET. THIS IS THE PLACE TO BE AT DUSK IN KEY WEST.

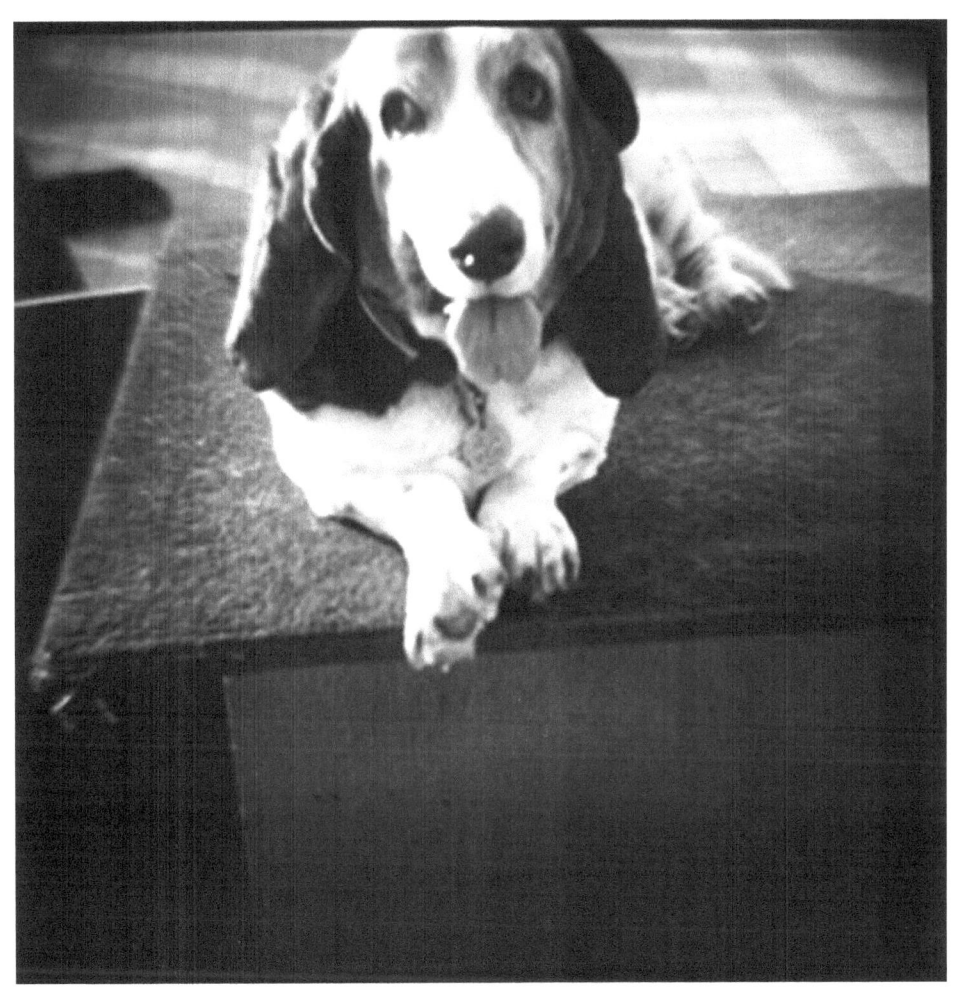

ROCKET THE PERFORMING DOG

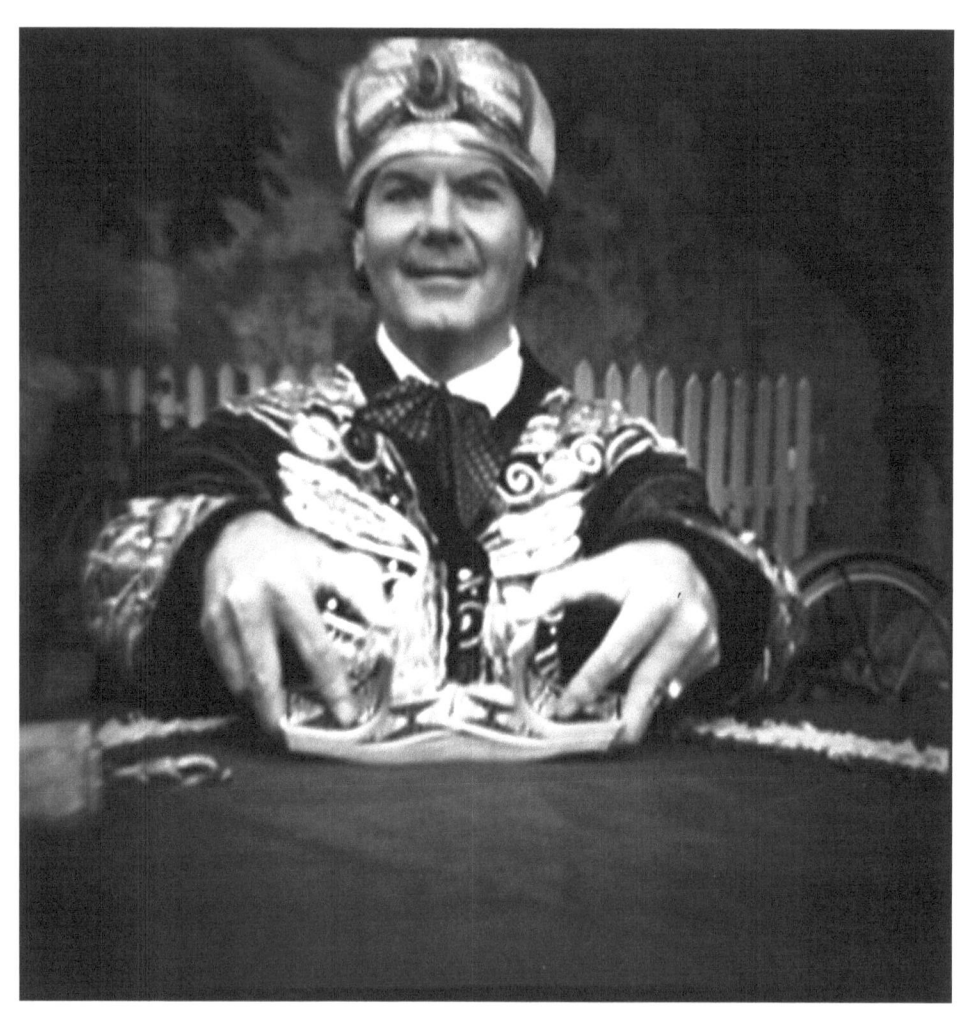

VISIONARY

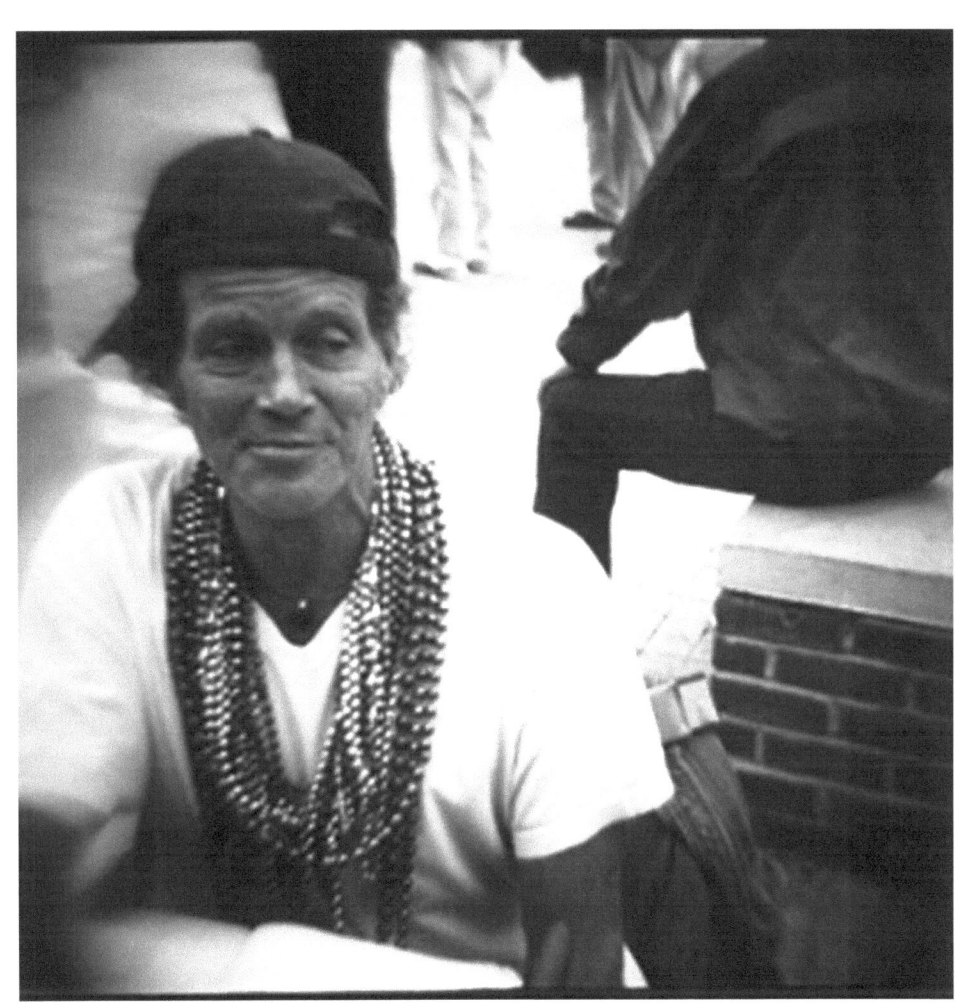

CRAFTSMAN

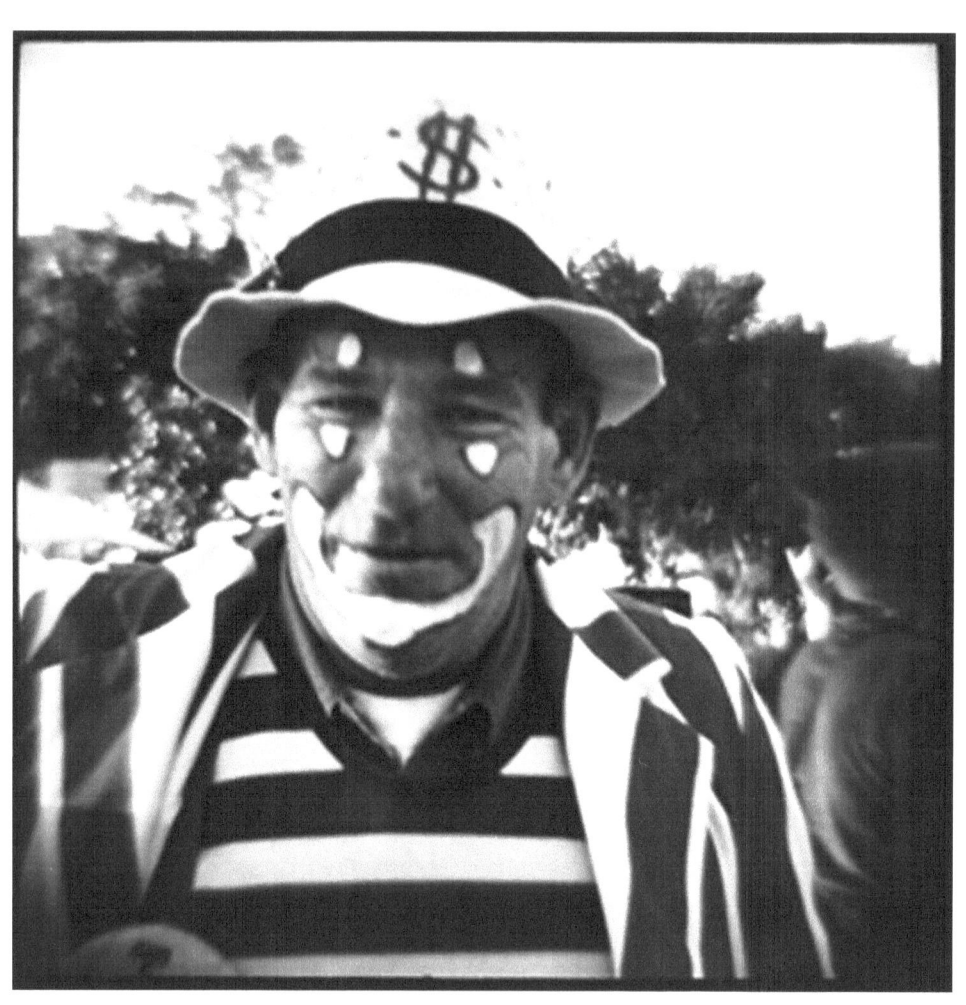

FLASH THE CLOWN

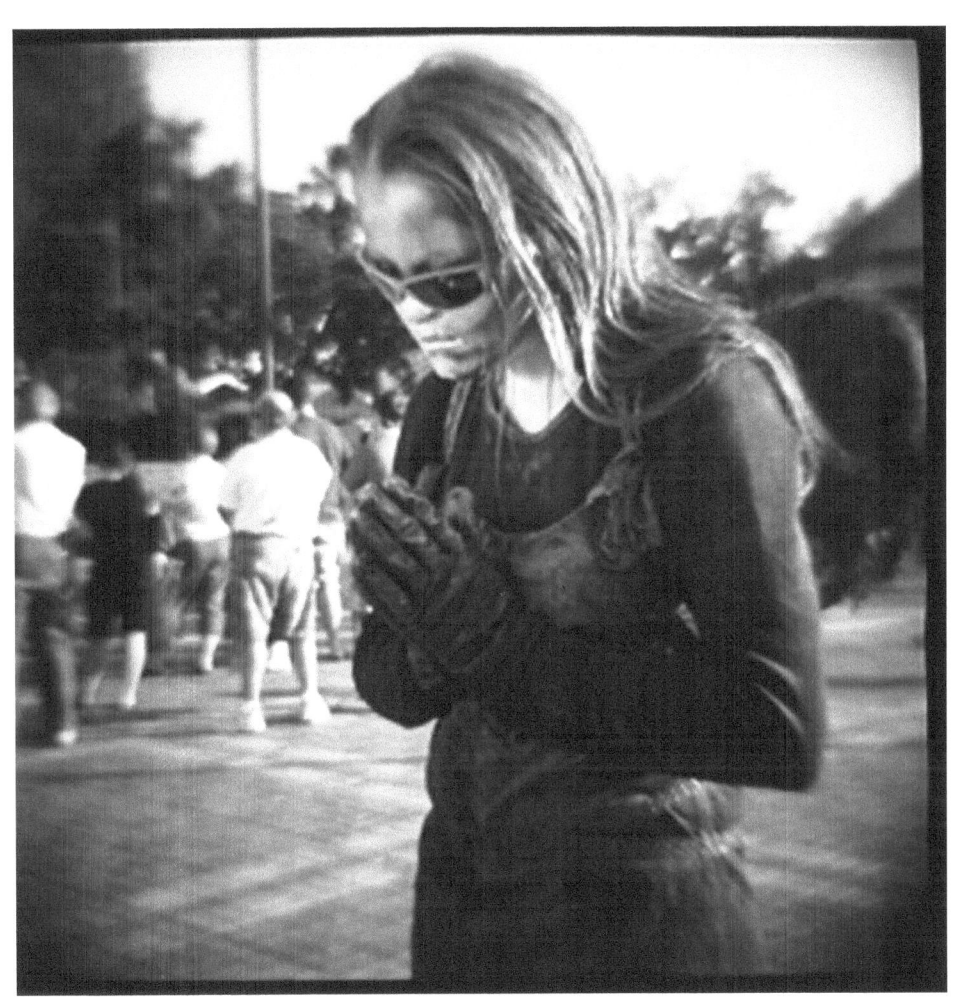

SILVER MIME

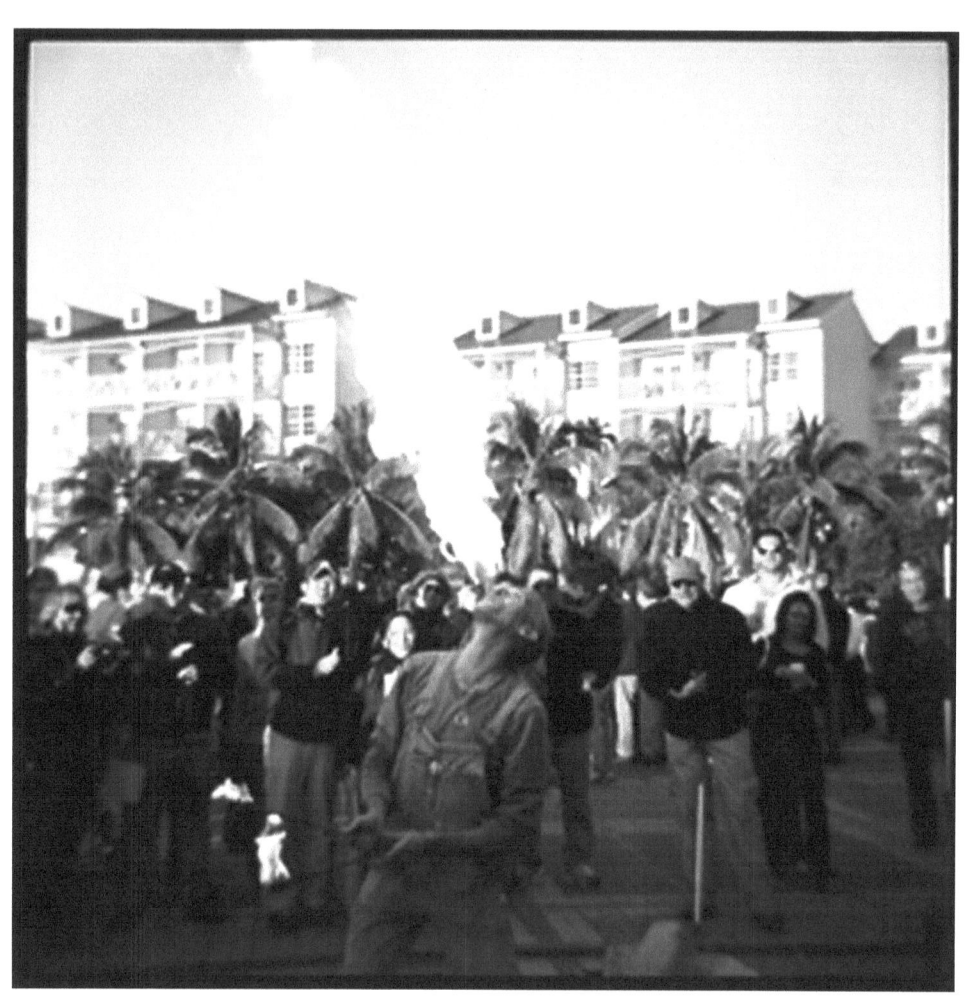

FIRE BREATHER

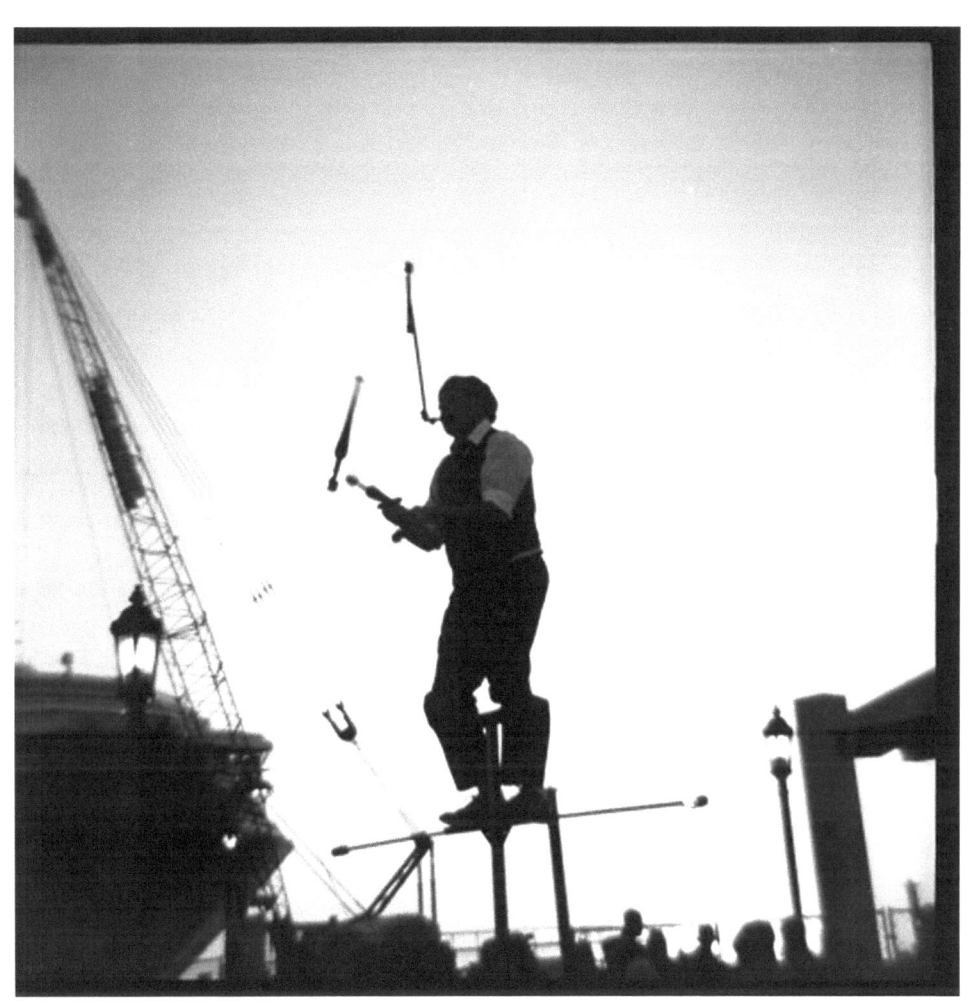

FIRE JUGGLER

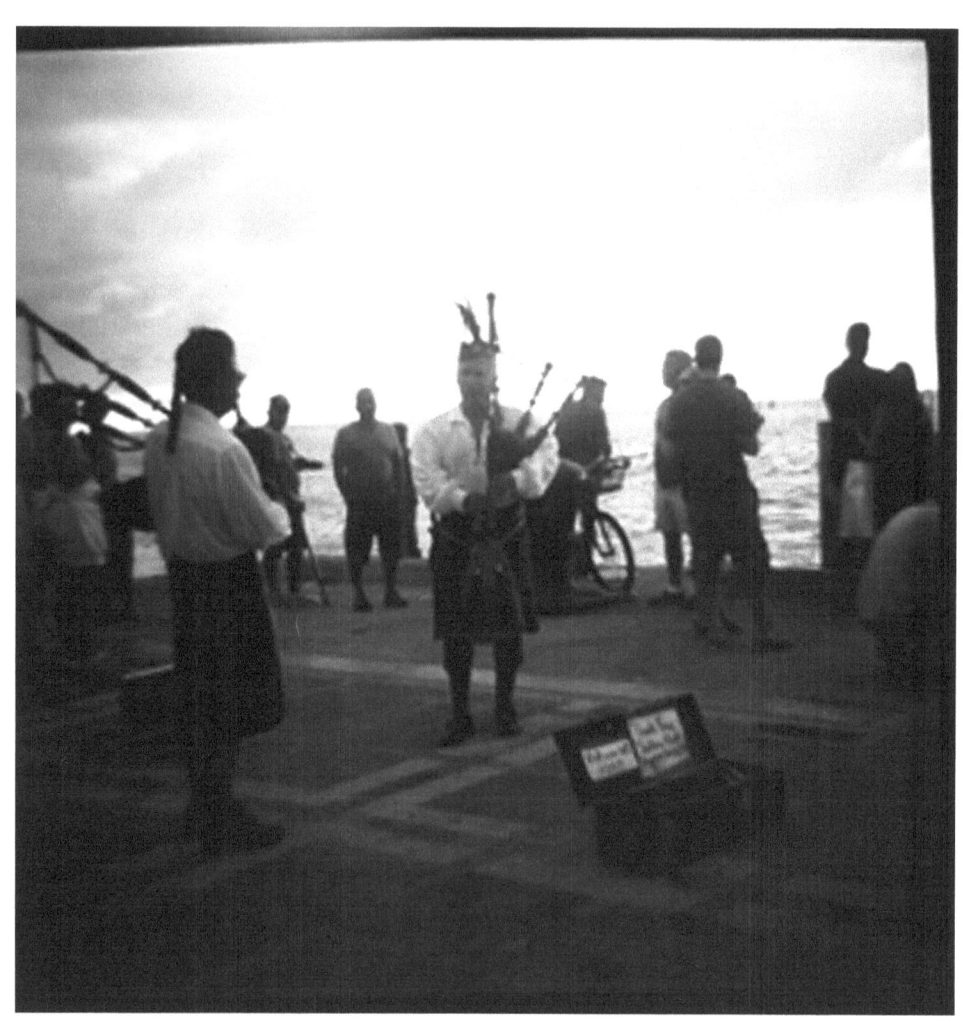

BAGPIPE PLAYERS

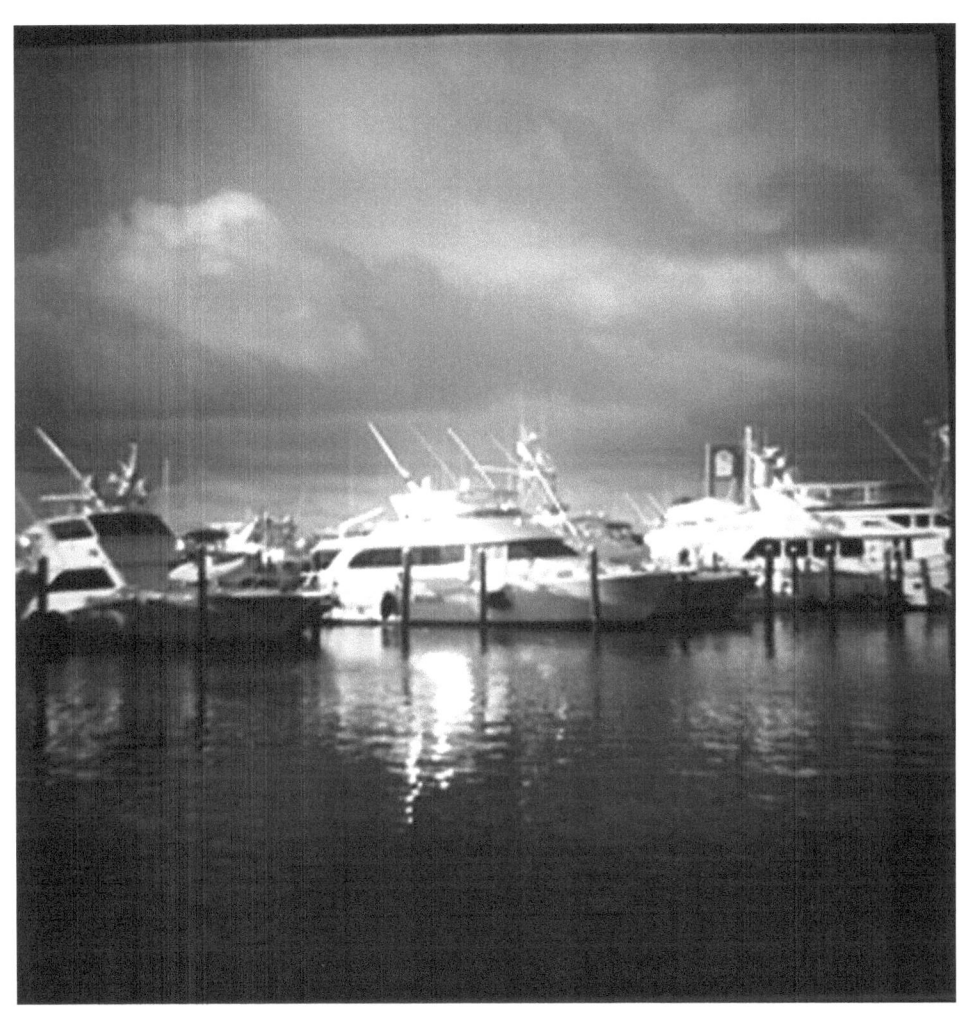

BOATS AT SUNSET

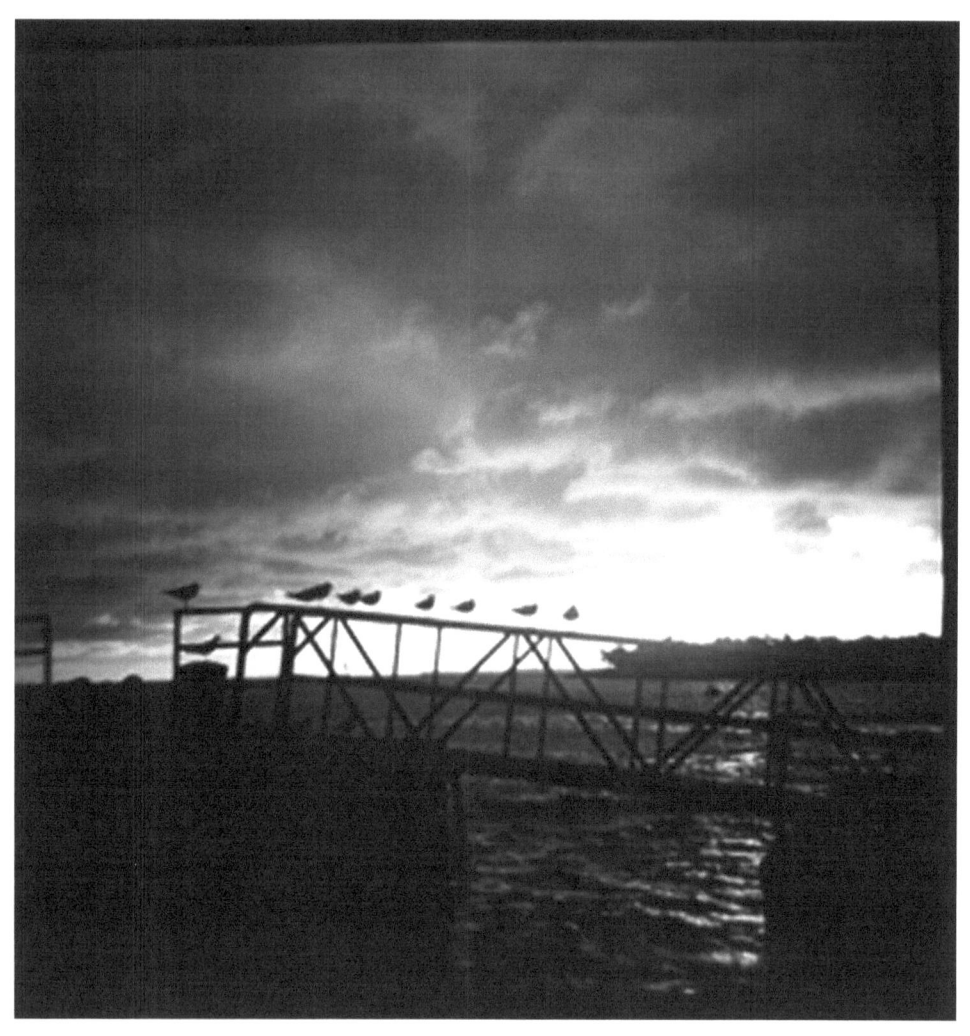

BIRDS ON A RAIL

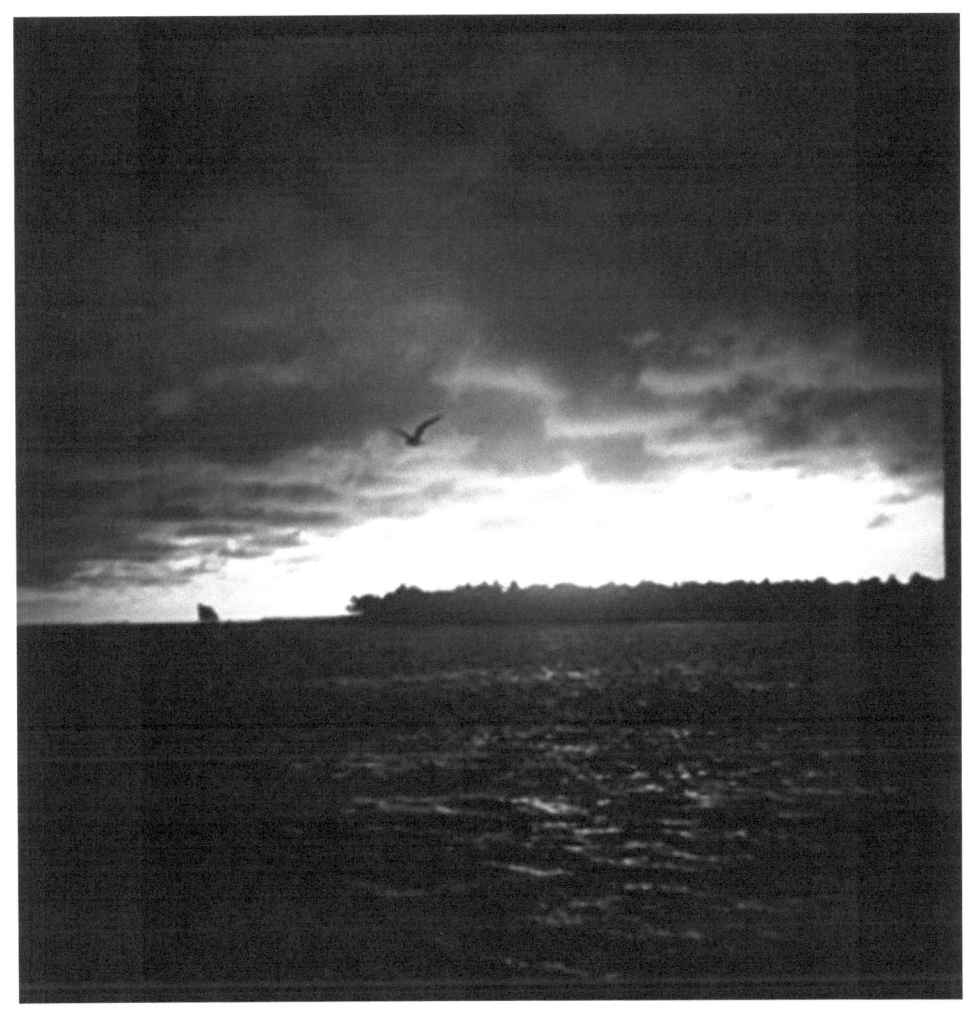

SUNSET

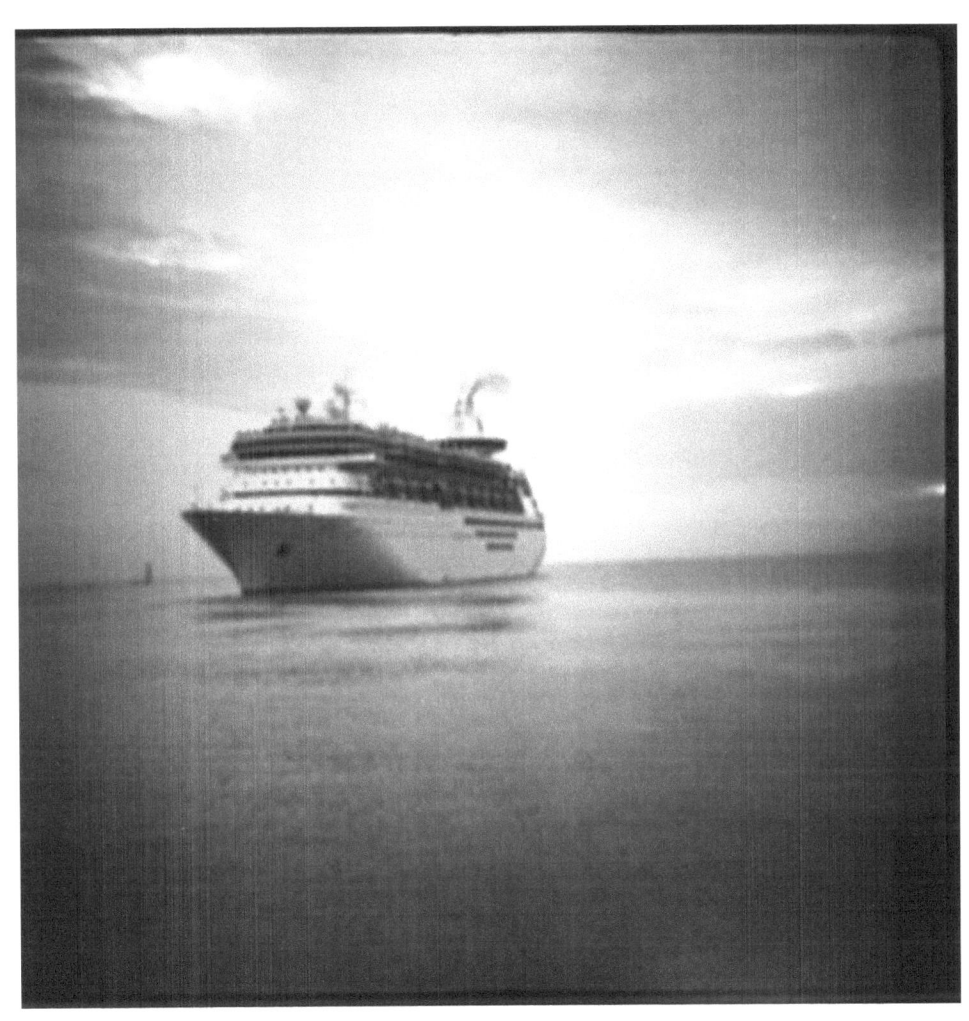

DEPARTING KEY WEST

ABOUT THE AUTHOR

Kathy Smith was born and raised in Sublimity, Oregon, and has lived in the Seattle area since 1982. Smith is a self-taught photographer with a passion for travel. Her equipment is a Diana Toy Camera (circa 1960.) The simple plastic lens produces less than sharp images with soft dreamlike effects.

Smith has exhibited her photographs in Washington and Oregon galleries and coffeehouses. In 2006, she published the first of the In Plain View Series of travel photography books, In Plain View Seattle, followed by Savannah in Plain View, and now Key West in Plain View. Smith is currently planning her next title, Santa Fe in Plain View.

KATHYSMITHPHOTOS.COM

IN PLAIN VIEW BOOKS
BY KATHY SMITH

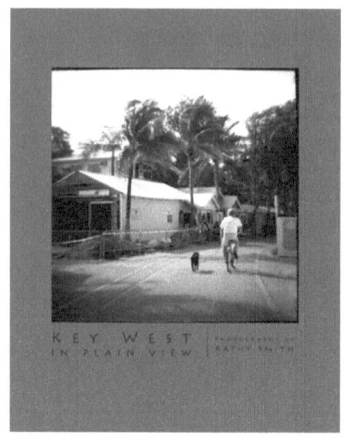

KEY WEST IN PLAIN VIEW
PHOTOGRAPHS BY KATHY SMITH
108 pages / 95 Photographs
Softbound / $19.95
Available at amazon.com and other retailers

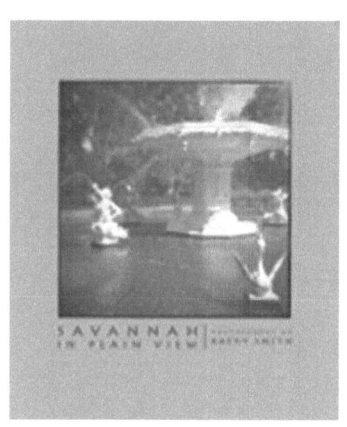

SAVANNAH IN PLAIN VIEW
PHOTOGRAPHS BY KATHY SMITH
128 pages / softbound / $19.95
Available at amazon.com and other retailers

"Kathy Smith has captured the essence of our charming city."
—Deborah Sullivan, Owner
"The Book" Gift Shop, Savannah, Georgia

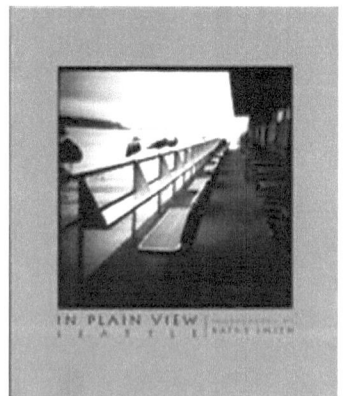

IN PLAIN VIEW SEATTLE
PHOTOGRAPHS BY KATHY SMITH
120 pages / softbound / $19.95
Available at amazon.com and other retailer

"These are the sorts of images that mythologize a city."
—Seattle Weekly

www.ingramcontent.com/pod-product-compliance
Lightning Source LLC
Chambersburg PA
CBHW051019180526
45172CB00002B/411